GO MATH

Grade 7

Assessment Resources

ISBN   978-0-544-06681-6

   6 7 8 9 10   0982   22 21 20 19 18 17 16 15 14
4500486618   B C D E F G

Contents

Introduction

Individual Student Profiles

Performance Tasks

Answer Sheets

Placement Test 1

Beginning-of-Year Diagnostic Test 5

Quizzes

Unit Tests and Performance Tasks

Benchmark Tests

Assessment Options

	Assessment Resources	Student Edition and Teacher's Edition	Online
			Personal Math Trainer Online Assessment and Intervention — Online homework assignment available — my.hrw.com
Diagnostic/ Entry Level	• Placement Test • Beginning-of-Year Diagnostic Test	• *Are You Ready?*	• Diagnostic Test • *Are You Ready?* Intervention and Enrichment
Formative/ Progress Monitoring	• Module Quizzes (Levels B, D)	• Your Turn • Math Talk • Reflect • Questioning Strategies • Essential Questions • Lesson Quizzes • *Ready to Go On?* Quizzes • Module Assessment Readiness	• *Ready to Go On?* Intervention and Enrichment • Online Homework • Module Assessment Readiness • Online Quizzes and Tests
Summative	• Unit Tests (Levels A, B, C, D) • Unit Performance Tasks • Quarterly Benchmark Tests • Mid-Year Test • End-of-Year Test	• Unit Assessment Readiness • Unit Performance Tasks	• Unit Assessment Readiness • Online Quizzes and Tests

Using the Assessment Resources

The *Assessment Resources* provides the following tests to assess mastery.

Diagnostic/ Entry Level	**Placement Test** • Use to assess prerequisite skills mastery before beginning the school year. • For students who require intervention, use the online *Are You Ready?* Intervention.	**Beginning-of-Year Diagnostic Test** • Use to assess knowledge of the key objectives that will be taught in the current school year. • Use as a baseline for a student's mastery of math concepts and skills, and to evaluate growth during the school year.
Formative/ Progress Monitoring	**Module Quizzes** • Use to assess mastery of the concepts and skills taught in the Modules. • Use Level D for students who are considerably below level and require modified materials. For all other students use Level B.	
Summative	**Unit Tests** • Use to assess mastery of the concepts and skills taught in the Units. • Level A: for students who are slightly below level • Level B: for students who are on level • Level C: for advanced students • Level D: for students who are considerably below level and require modified materials	**Benchmark Tests** • Use for test prep. • There are four Benchmark Tests: two quarterly tests, the Mid-Year Test, and the End-of-Year Test.
	Performance Tasks • Use to provide alternate assessment at the end of each Unit. • These tasks are accessible to all students and suitable to be completed in a classroom. • Before starting the Performance Task, provide students with the *Scoring Rubric for Students* to establish the expectations and scoring rubrics for the task. Use the *Teacher's Guide Scoring Rubric* to assess students' work and their competency with applying the Mathematical Practices.	

Placement Test

Individual Student Profile

The Proficient? column provides a snapshot of a student's mastery of previous grade-level standards.

Each Student Edition Module begins with *Are You Ready?*, a tool to assess whether students have the prerequisite skills needed to be successful. *Are You Ready?* Intervention is also available online.

Name _____ Date _____ Class _____

COMMON CORE	Placement Test Items	Proficient? Yes/No	COMMON CORE	Placement Test Items	Proficient? Yes/No
6.EE.1	23, 24		6.NS.6	1	
6.EE.2	37		6.NS.6a	2	
6.EE.2a	26		6.NS.6b	19, 33	
6.EE.2b	26		6.NS.6c	2, 19	
6.EE.3	27, 37		6.NS.7a	3, 4	
6.EE.4	27		6.NS.7b	3, 4	
6.EE.5	25, 31, 32		6.NS.8	19, 33	
6.EE.6	25, 26, 31, 32		6.RP.1	12	
6.EE.7	25, 30, 32		6.RP.2	13	
6.EE.8	31		6.RP.3	9, 13, 18	
6.EE.9	20, 21, 22		6.RP.3a	9, 12	
6.G.1	28, 29, 36		6.RP.3b	13, 18	
6.G.2	30, 35		6.RP.3c	14, 16	
6.G.3	33		6.RP.3d	15, 17	
6.G.4	34		6.SP.2	38	
6.NS.1	5, 8		6.SP.3	38	
6.NS.2	10		6.SP.5a	40	
6.NS.3	11		6.SP.5b	40	
6.NS.4	6, 7		6.SP.5c	37, 38, 39	
6.NS.5	2		6.SP.5d	37, 38	

Beginning-of-Year Diagnostic Test
Individual Student Profile

The Proficient? column provides a snapshot of a student's knowledge of key objectives that will be taught in this grade. The Diagnostic Test can be used as a baseline for a student's mastery of objectives and to evaluate growth.

Name _____ Date _____ Class _____

COMMON CORE	Student Edition Modules	Diagnostic Test Items	Proficient? Yes/No
7.EE.1	6	9, 90	
7.EE.2	6	84	
7.EE.3	1, 3, 4, 5, 6	6, 7, 37, 40, 50, 55, 62, 65, 68, 71, 73, 76, 78, 84	
7.EE.4a	6	26, 34, 48, 60	
7.EE.4b	6, 7	33, 49, 52, 62, 69, 79	
7.G.1	8	11, 14, 24, 64, 66, 72	
7.G.2	8	87	
7.G.3	8	85	
7.G.4	9	18, 39, 43, 51, 67	
7.G.5	8	36, 46, 47	
7.G.6	9	16, 20, 31, 35, 38, 59, 61, 70, 81	
7.NS.1	3	71	
7.NS.1a	1	83	
7.NS.1c	1	83	
7.NS.1d	1, 3,	1, 6	
7.NS.2	3	82	
7.NS.2a	4	3	
7.NS.2b	2	2	
7.NS.2c	3	74	
7.NS.2d	3	4, 12, 27	
7.NS.3	1, 3, 4	6, 7, 73, 74	
7.RP.1	4	8, 10, 13, 22, 78	
7.RP.2	4	77, 80	
7.RP.2a	4	19	

Beginning-of-Year Diagnostic Test

Individual Student Profile (continued)

Name _____ Date _____ Class _____

COMMON CORE	Student Edition Modules	Diagnostic Test Items	Proficient? Yes/No
7.RP.2b	4, 9	5, 19, 43	
7.RP.2d	4	19	
7.RP.3	3, 4, 5	7, 15, 19, 37, 40, 42, 50, 55, 68, 80	
7.SP.1	10	23, 32, 41	
7.SP.2	10	32, 41	
7.SP.3	11	29, 44, 45, 54, 57	
7.SP.4	11	29, 44, 45, 54, 57	
7.SP.5	13	25, 28, 63	
7.SP.6	9, 12, 13	17, 53, 56, 58	
7.SP.7	13	63	
7.SP.7a	9, 13	21, 28, 30, 56	
7.SP.7b	9	17	
7.SP.8a	13	30, 86	
7.SP.8b	13	30, 88	
7.SP.8c	13	75, 88	

Mathematical Practices

Performance Tasks

Teacher's Guide

Performance Tasks provide an alternate way for teachers to assess students' mastery of concepts. This method of assessment requires the student to create answers by using critical thinking skills.

Through observation or analysis of students' responses, teachers can determine what the students know, do not know, and whether the students have any misconceptions.

Assigning Performance Tasks

Discuss with students what is expected before they start the Performance Task. Provide the *Scoring Rubric for Students* to help them understand the scoring criteria.

- Encourage discussion of new ideas and viability of other students' reasoning and work.

- Encourage multiple approaches, and emphasize that not just one answer is correct.

- Encourage students to initiate a plan.

- Encourage students to manage, analyze, and synthesize information.

- Encourage students to use appropriate tools and math models to solve the problems, and remind students to attend to precision.

Use the *Teacher's Guide Scoring Rubric* to help assess the complex learning outcomes.

Performance Tasks

Scoring Rubric for Students

What you are expected to do:

☐ Make a plan. If the plan does not work, change it until it does work.

☐ Use accurate reasoning to represent the problem.

☐ Fully explain the steps that you used to find the solution.

☐ Use different methods and models to help you find the solution.

☐ Use appropriate tools such as rulers, geometry tools, and calculators.

☐ Use clear language to explain your answers. Check that your answers are accurate.

☐ Look for patterns and explain your reasoning using different representations such as symbols, words, or graphs.

☐ Find efficient ways to solve the problems, and explain general rules clearly.

Your teacher will need to see all your work. Be sure to include the following:

☐ Drawings, tables, and graphs to support your answers.

☐ Clearly written sentences to explain your reasoning.

☐ All the steps in your solution.

☐ The answer; check that it is reasonable and answers the question.

Performance Tasks

Teacher's Guide Scoring Rubric

Mathematical Practices	Level 4	Level 3	Level 2	Level 1
Make sense of problems and persevere in solving them.	Student makes a plan and follows it, or adjusts it to obtain a solution.	Student makes a viable plan but implementation has minor flaws.	Student makes a plan, but it has major flaws that the student is unable to address.	Student shows no evidence of making a plan.
Reason abstractly and quantitatively.	Student uses accurate reasoning to represent the problem.	Student reasoning shows a minor flaw.	Student reasoning is missing a critical step.	Student shows little evidence of mathematical reasoning.
Construct viable arguments and critique the reasoning of others.	Student fully explains the steps that lead to the conclusion.	Student skips a step in the explanation.	Student has missing or out-of-sequence steps in the explanation.	Student makes no attempt to explain the steps used.
Model mathematics [using graphs, diagrams, tables, formulas].	Student uses appropriate models and implements them correctly.	Student chooses an appropriate model, but makes minor error(s) in implementation.	Student chooses a model but is unable to relate it effectively to the problem.	Student is unable to model the relationship.
Use appropriate tools [e.g., ruler, paper/pencil, technology] strategically.	Student chooses appropriate tools and uses them effectively.	Student chooses an appropriate tool, but makes minor error(s) in its use.	Student chooses an appropriate tool, but cannot apply it properly to the problem.	Student chooses an inappropriate tool or none at all.
Attend to precision.	Student uses clear language and accurate calculations.	Student uses some vocabulary incorrectly and/or makes minor error(s) in calculations.	Student use of language is confusing and/or makes errors in calculations.	Student does not provide an explanation; calculations are inaccurate.
Look for and make use of structure.	Student finds and uses patterns and processes, and expresses them accurately.	Student finds and uses patterns and processes, but makes minor error(s) in expressing them.	Student finds patterns and processes, but cannot apply them successfully.	Student is unable to find patterns and processes that are appropriate.
Look for and express regularity in repeated reasoning.	Student finds shortcuts and/or generalizations and expresses them clearly.	Student finds shortcuts and/or generalizations, but makes minor errors.	Student finds a shortcut or generalization, but does not represent it effectively.	Student is unable to find shortcuts and/or generalizations.

Multiple-Choice Answer Sheet

Test Title _____

1. Ⓐ Ⓑ Ⓒ Ⓓ
2. Ⓐ Ⓑ Ⓒ Ⓓ
3. Ⓐ Ⓑ Ⓒ Ⓓ
4. Ⓐ Ⓑ Ⓒ Ⓓ
5. Ⓐ Ⓑ Ⓒ Ⓓ

6. Ⓐ Ⓑ Ⓒ Ⓓ
7. Ⓐ Ⓑ Ⓒ Ⓓ
8. Ⓐ Ⓑ Ⓒ Ⓓ
9. Ⓐ Ⓑ Ⓒ Ⓓ
10. Ⓐ Ⓑ Ⓒ Ⓓ

11. Ⓐ Ⓑ Ⓒ Ⓓ
12. Ⓐ Ⓑ Ⓒ Ⓓ
13. Ⓐ Ⓑ Ⓒ Ⓓ
14. Ⓐ Ⓑ Ⓒ Ⓓ
15. Ⓐ Ⓑ Ⓒ Ⓓ

16. Ⓐ Ⓑ Ⓒ Ⓓ
17. Ⓐ Ⓑ Ⓒ Ⓓ
18. Ⓐ Ⓑ Ⓒ Ⓓ
19. Ⓐ Ⓑ Ⓒ Ⓓ
20. Ⓐ Ⓑ Ⓒ Ⓓ

21. Ⓐ Ⓑ Ⓒ Ⓓ
22. Ⓐ Ⓑ Ⓒ Ⓓ
23. Ⓐ Ⓑ Ⓒ Ⓓ
24. Ⓐ Ⓑ Ⓒ Ⓓ
25. Ⓐ Ⓑ Ⓒ Ⓓ

26. Ⓐ Ⓑ Ⓒ Ⓓ
27. Ⓐ Ⓑ Ⓒ Ⓓ
28. Ⓐ Ⓑ Ⓒ Ⓓ
29. Ⓐ Ⓑ Ⓒ Ⓓ
30. Ⓐ Ⓑ Ⓒ Ⓓ

31. Ⓐ Ⓑ Ⓒ Ⓓ
32. Ⓐ Ⓑ Ⓒ Ⓓ
33. Ⓐ Ⓑ Ⓒ Ⓓ
34. Ⓐ Ⓑ Ⓒ Ⓓ
35. Ⓐ Ⓑ Ⓒ Ⓓ

36. Ⓐ Ⓑ Ⓒ Ⓓ
37. Ⓐ Ⓑ Ⓒ Ⓓ
38. Ⓐ Ⓑ Ⓒ Ⓓ
39. Ⓐ Ⓑ Ⓒ Ⓓ
40. Ⓐ Ⓑ Ⓒ Ⓓ

41. Ⓐ Ⓑ Ⓒ Ⓓ
42. Ⓐ Ⓑ Ⓒ Ⓓ
43. Ⓐ Ⓑ Ⓒ Ⓓ
44. Ⓐ Ⓑ Ⓒ Ⓓ
45. Ⓐ Ⓑ Ⓒ Ⓓ

46. Ⓐ Ⓑ Ⓒ Ⓓ
47. Ⓐ Ⓑ Ⓒ Ⓓ
48. Ⓐ Ⓑ Ⓒ Ⓓ
49. Ⓐ Ⓑ Ⓒ Ⓓ
50. Ⓐ Ⓑ Ⓒ Ⓓ

Multiple-Choice Answer Sheet

Test Title _____

51. (A) (B) (C) (D)
52. (A) (B) (C) (D)
53. (A) (B) (C) (D)
54. (A) (B) (C) (D)
55. (A) (B) (C) (D)

56. (A) (B) (C) (D)
57. (A) (B) (C) (D)
58. (A) (B) (C) (D)
59. (A) (B) (C) (D)
60. (A) (B) (C) (D)

61. (A) (B) (C) (D)
62. (A) (B) (C) (D)
63. (A) (B) (C) (D)
64. (A) (B) (C) (D)
65. (A) (B) (C) (D)

66. (A) (B) (C) (D)
67. (A) (B) (C) (D)
68. (A) (B) (C) (D)
69. (A) (B) (C) (D)
70. (A) (B) (C) (D)

71. (A) (B) (C) (D)
72. (A) (B) (C) (D)
73. (A) (B) (C) (D)
74. (A) (B) (C) (D)
75. (A) (B) (C) (D)

76. (A) (B) (C) (D)
77. (A) (B) (C) (D)
78. (A) (B) (C) (D)
79. (A) (B) (C) (D)
80. (A) (B) (C) (D)

81. (A) (B) (C) (D)
82. (A) (B) (C) (D)
83. (A) (B) (C) (D)
84. (A) (B) (C) (D)
85. (A) (B) (C) (D)

86. (A) (B) (C) (D)
87. (A) (B) (C) (D)
88. (A) (B) (C) (D)
89. (A) (B) (C) (D)
90. (A) (B) (C) (D)

91. (A) (B) (C) (D)
92. (A) (B) (C) (D)
93. (A) (B) (C) (D)
94. (A) (B) (C) (D)
95. (A) (B) (C) (D)

96. (A) (B) (C) (D)
97. (A) (B) (C) (D)
98. (A) (B) (C) (D)
99. (A) (B) (C) (D)
100. (A) (B) (C) (D)

Name _____ Date _____ Class _____

Placement Test

1. To which set or sets below does the number $-\dfrac{7}{8}$ belong?

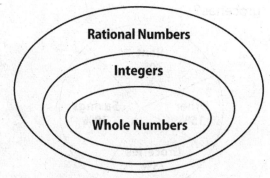

   A whole numbers only

   B rational numbers only

   C integers and rational numbers only

   D whole numbers, integers, and rational numbers

2. Which of the following points is graphed at the opposite of –4 on the number line below?

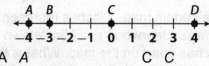

   A A

   B B

   C C

   D D

3. Jamal plotted points on a number line at the four values below.

$$0.27, \ -\frac{1}{4}, \ 1.1, \ \frac{5}{3}$$

   Which of these values is farthest from zero?

   A 0.27

   B $-\dfrac{1}{4}$

   C 1.1

   D $\dfrac{5}{3}$

4. Harriet recorded outdoor temperatures as –7°C, –2°C, and 1°C. Which of the following correctly compares the three temperatures?

   A –7 < 1 < –2

   B 1 < –2 < –7

   C –2 < 1 < –7

   D –7 < –2 < 1

5. Which of the following is equivalent to the expression below?

$$\frac{2}{9} \times \frac{3}{4}$$

   A $\dfrac{2}{9} \div \dfrac{3}{4}$

   B $\dfrac{3}{4} \div \dfrac{2}{9}$

   C $\dfrac{2}{9} \div \dfrac{4}{3}$

   D $\dfrac{9}{2} \div \dfrac{4}{3}$

6. What is the greatest common factor of 12 and 48?

   A 12

   B 24

   C 36

   D 48

7. What is the least common multiple of 5 and 12?

   A 24

   B 30

   C 36

   D 60

8. Abby is making frozen popsicles using $5\dfrac{3}{4}$ cups of fruit juice and $1\dfrac{3}{4}$ cups of water. Abby mixes the fruit juice and water together. She will then pour the mixture into popsicle molds. Each mold will hold $\dfrac{1}{2}$ cup. How many popsicles can Abby make?

   A 7

   B 15

   C 20

   D 24

9. Zoe is making a quilt using 15 red squares and 30 green squares. Which combination shows the same ratio of red squares to green squares?

   A 3 red squares to 6 green squares

   B 6 red squares to 3 green squares

   C 5 red squares to 12 green squares

   D 12 red squares to 5 green squares

Placement Test

10. Last year, a local amusement park received 286,758 visitors. It was open every day of the year except 7 holidays. What was the average number of visitors to the park per day?

    A 786 visitors   C 957 visitors

    B 801 visitors   D 1,204 visitors

11. Dennis ran a mile in 593.7 seconds. Martina ran a mile in 573.36 seconds. What was the difference in their running times?

    A 5.14 s   C 20.34 s

    B 6.01 s   D 26.01 s

12. In Ellen's math class, there are 2 boys for every 3 girls. Which of the following could be the ratio of boys to girls in the class?

    A $\frac{17}{21}$ C $\frac{7}{14}$

    B $\frac{14}{21}$ D $\frac{11}{17}$

13. Seth bought a 12-ounce jar of peanut butter for $3.60. What is the unit price?

    A $0.03/oz   C $3.00/oz

    B $0.30/oz   D $3.03/oz

14. What percent of the rectangle below is shaded?

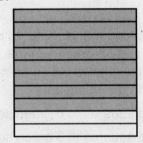

    A 20%   C 40%

    B 30%   D 80%

15. Yvette measured the length of her driveway to be 5 meters long. Which of these is an equivalent measurement?

    A 0.07 mi   C 16.4 ft

    B 15.5 yd   D 585 in.

16. Jason's budget is shown in the circle graph below. His total monthly budget is $3,000. How much does Jason spend on groceries?

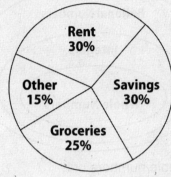

    A $25   C $450

    B $150   D $750

17. Mary bought 10 quarts of juice at the grocery. How many gallons of juice did she buy?

    A 1.4 gal   C 3.5 gal

    B 2.5 gal   D 4.5 gal

18. On a certain map, 3 inches represents 15 miles. Briarwood and Middletown are 5 inches apart on the map. What is the actual distance between Briarwood and Middletown?

    A 25 mi   C 50 mi

    B 30 mi   D 75 mi

Use the graph for 19–20.

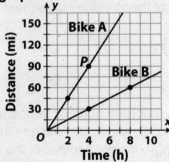

19. What are the coordinates of point P?

    A (4, 3)   C (4, 90)

    B (4, 30)   D (40, 90)

Name _____ Date _____ Class_____

Placement Test

20. What is the independent variable?

    A Bike A   C time

    B Bike B   D distance

Use the table for 21–22.

Machine Rental Charges

Hours, x	3	5	7
Charge, y ($)	51	85	119

21. Which equation expresses y in terms of x?

    A $y = 17x$ C $x = 51y$

    B $y = 25x$ D $x = 85y$

22. What is the charge for renting a machine for 3.5 hours?

    A $51.50   C $65.50

    B $59.50   D $86.50

23. What are all the factors of 15?

    A 1, 3, 5

    B 1, 3, 5, 10

    C 1, 2, 3, 5, 10

    D 1, 3, 5, 15

24. What is the value of the expression below?

$$675 - (15 - 12)^3 \div 3$$

    A 216   C 666

    B 224   D 678

25. On a farm, there are c cows and 15 sheep. There are 4 more sheep than cows. Which equation represents the situation?

    A $c = 15 + 4$

    B $c = 15 - 4$

    C $c = 4 - 15$

    D $c = 4 \times 15$

26. Write an algebraic expression for the phrase below.

8 more than three times a number n

    A $3 + 8n$ C $3n - 8$

    B $8n - 3$ D $3n + 8$

27. Which of the following expressions is equivalent to the expression below?

$$4(2x + 11 - x)$$

    A $8x + 11$ C $2x - 11$

    B $x + 22$ D $4x + 44$

28. A triangle has an area of 369.25 square inches. The height of the triangle is 42.2 inches. What is the length of the base of the triangle?

    A 17.5 in.   C 42.7 in.

    B 35 in.   D 56 in.

29. A parallelogram has a base of 9 centimeters and a height of 21 centimeters. What is the area of the parallelogram?

    A 30 cm^2 C 189 cm^2

    B 94.5 cm^2 D 567 cm^2

30. A rectangular prism has a volume of 285.6 cubic feet. The prism is 12 feet long and 3.4 feet wide. What is the height of the prism?

    A 7 ft   C 19 ft

    B 15 ft   D 22 ft

31. Which inequality is shown on the number line below?

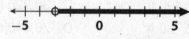

    A $p < -3$ C $p > -3$

    B $p \le -3$ D $p \ge -3$

32. Mariah bought a shirt for $28.50 and a belt. The total cost was $45.50. Which of the following equations can be used to find the cost of the belt?

    A $28.50 + b = 45.50$

    B $45.50 + b = 28.50$

    C $b = 28.50 - 45.50$

    D $b = 28.50 \times 45.50$

Name _____ Date _____ Class_____

Placement Test

33. What is the distance between points A and B on the grid?

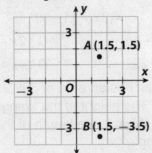

  A   3 units   C   5 units
  B   4.5 units   D   5.5 units

34. Charlene is wrapping the box below. How much wrapping paper will she need?

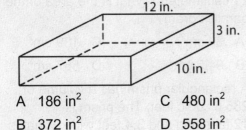

  A   186 in²   C   480 in²
  B   372 in²   D   558 in²

35. A shipping container in the shape of a rectangular prism is 60 feet long, $45\frac{1}{2}$ feet wide, and 14 feet tall. What is the volume of the shipping container?

  A   2,400 ft³   C   38,220 ft³
  B   2,730 ft³   D   76,440 ft³

36. What is the area of the polygon shown below?

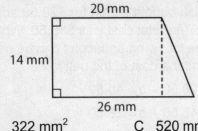

  A   322 mm²   C   520 mm²
  B   364 mm²   D   584 mm²

37. What is the median of the data represented in the box plot below?

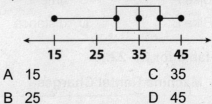

  A   15   C   35
  B   25   D   45

38. What is the mode of the data represented in the dot plot below?

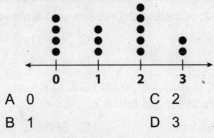

  A   0   C   2
  B   1   D   3

39. Lisa read 46 pages on Sunday, 15 pages on Monday, and 19 pages on Tuesday. Which of the following is closest to the mean number of pages she read over the three-day period?

  A   19 pages   C   27 pages
  B   21 pages   D   35 pages

40. The histogram below shows the number of hours per year students in Mr. Hopper's class do volunteer work. How many students do volunteer work between 21 and 30 hours per year?

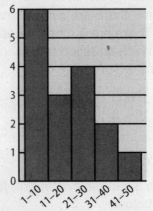

  A   2 students   C   4 students
  B   3 students   D   6 students

Beginning-of-Year Diagnostic Test

1. At 7 P.M. the temperature was 5°F. At midnight the temperature was –7°F. What was the change in temperature?

   A –12°F   C 5°F

   B –7°F   D 12°F

2. What is the product of –12(–5)?

   A –60   C 48

   B –48   D 60

3. What is true about the relationship between miles and gallons?

gallons	2	4	6	8
miles	30	60	90	120

   A There is no relationship between miles and gallons.

   B There is a proportional relationship between miles and gallons.

   C There is a 1 to 15 relationship between miles and gallons.

   D There is a 30 to 1 relationship between miles and gallons.

4. Which decimal is equivalent to $\frac{4}{20}$?

   A 0.2   C 1.4

   B 0.6   D 4.2

5. At the farmers' market, you can buy 3 jars of honey for $12, 6 jars of honey for $24, or 9 jars of honey for $36. What is the constant of proportionality for buying jars of honey?

   A 3   C 6

   B 4   D 12

6. Andrella makes bead bracelets. Each bracelet is 7 inches long. Andrella has a 67-inch length of beaded string. How many necklaces can she make?

   A 7 necklaces   C 10 necklaces

   B 9 necklaces   D 11 necklaces

7. The ground temperature at sea level is 60°F. For every 100-foot increase in elevation, the temperature rises $\frac{1}{10}$ of one degree. At an altitude of 2,000 feet, what will be the likely temperature?

   A 58°F   C 72°F

   B 62°F   D 80°F

8. Tamara walked $\frac{3}{4}$ mile in $\frac{1}{2}$ hour. Which of the following represents the unit rate that Tamara walked?

   A $\frac{1}{2}$ mi/h   C $\frac{3}{4}$ mi/h

   B $\frac{2}{3}$ mi/h   D $1\frac{1}{2}$ mi/h

9. Simplify $\frac{1}{2}(2a + b) - (4a + b)$.

   A $-3a - \frac{1}{2}b$ C $-3a + \frac{3}{2}b$

   B $-2a + 2b$ D $-3a - b$

10. Jay spent $6.40 to buy 4 muffins. How much will 9 muffins cost?

    A $12.03   C $14.40

    B $12.80   D $144.00

11. A reduced scale drawing of a rectangle measures 12 inches by 16 inches. The scale factor is $\frac{1}{4}$. What is the size of the original rectangle?

    A 3 in. × 4 in.   C 36 in. × 48 in.

    B 16 in. × 20 in.   D 48 in. × 64 in.

12. Which fraction is equivalent to –0.12?

    A $-\frac{3}{25}$ C $-\frac{4}{25}$

    B $-\frac{7}{50}$ D $-\frac{6}{25}$

13. The cost of 2 pounds of coffee is $17.95. To the nearest dollar, what is the cost of 5 pounds of coffee?

   A $34   C $45

   B $36   D $90

14. On a map, the distance between two cities is 5.25 inches. The map scale is 1 in.:25 mi To the nearest mile, what is the actual distance between the two cities?

   A 13 mi   C 125 mi

   B 30 mi   D 131 mi

15. Patti got a new part-time job. Her hourly wage increased from $10.50 to $12.39. What was the percent increase in Patti's hourly wage?

   A 1.8%   C 18%

   B 15.25%   D 189%

16. To the nearest cubic centimeter, what is the volume of the prism below?

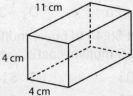

   A 19 cm^3 C 88 cm^3

   B 44 cm^3 D 176 cm^3

17. A bag contains 12 blue marbles, 5 red marbles, and 3 green marbles. Jonas selects a marble and then returns it to the bag before selecting a marble again. If Jonas selects a blue marble 4 out of 20 times, what is the experimental probability that the next marble he selects will be blue?

   A .02%   C 20%

   B 2%   D 200%

18. The circumference of a circle is 36π inches. What is the radius of this circle?

   A 9 in.   C 18 in.

   B 12 in.   D 36 in.

19. Which equation is represented by the graph below?

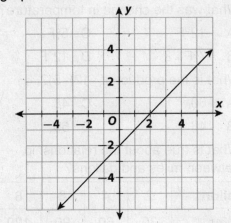

   A $y + 2 = x$

   B $y + 1 = x$

   C $y - 1 = x$

   D $y - 2 = x$

20. To the nearest square inch, what is the surface area of the square pyramid below?

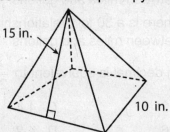

   A 175 in^2 C 400 in^2

   B 200 in^2 D 700 in^2

21. Cybil flips a coin and rolls a fair number cube at the same time. What is the probability that she will toss tails and roll a number less than 3?

   A $\dfrac{1}{6}$ C $\dfrac{2}{5}$

   B $\dfrac{1}{3}$ D $\dfrac{1}{2}$

22. The Rogers family drove 220 miles in 5.5 hours. How many miles would they drive at this same rate in 4 hours?

   A 88 mi   C 160 mi

   B 147 mi   D 176 mi

Beginning-of-Year Diagnostic Test

23. Your school is choosing a new school mascot to represent all team sports. Which group should you ask to get a random sample of student opinion?

    A students on the basketball team

    B every 10th student that enters the cafeteria

    C the first 20 seniors at the library

    D students on the cheerleading squad

24. A rectangle is 14 inches long and 4 inches wide. A smaller, similar rectangle is 2 inches wide. To the nearest inch, what is the length of the smaller rectangle?

    A $3\frac{1}{2}$ in.   C 8 in.

    B 7 in.   D 28 in.

25. There are 30 colored marbles inside a bag. Six marbles are yellow, 9 are red, 7 are white, and 8 are blue. One is drawn at random. Which color is most likely to be chosen?

    A white   C blue

    B red   D yellow

26. Which table represents the same linear relationship as the equation $y = 2x + 6$?

    A

x	0	1	2	5
y	6	7	8	10

    B

x	2	3	4	5
y	8	9	10	11

    C

x	2	3	4	5
y	10	12	14	16

    D

x	2	3	4	5
y	16	18	20	22

27. Evan's dog weighs $15\frac{3}{8}$ pounds. What is this weight written as a decimal?

    A 15.125 lb   C 15.385 lb

    B 15.375 lb   D 15.625 lb

28. The spinner below is divided into sections that are red, green, or blue. What is the probability that the spinner will land on red or green?

    A $\frac{1}{4}$ C $\frac{1}{2}$

    B $\frac{3}{8}$ D $\frac{5}{8}$

29. Based on the dot plots below, which of the following is a true statement?

    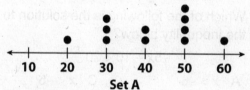

    Set A

    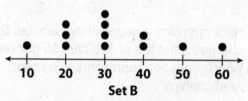

    Set B

    A Set B has the greater mode.

    B Set A has more items than set B.

    C Set A is more symmetric than set B.

    D Set B has the greater range.

30. For a trip, Eli packed 3 shirts, 3 pairs of pants, and 2 pairs of shoes. How many different outfits can Eli make?

    A 6 outfits   C 9 outfits

    B 8 outfits   D 18 outfits

Beginning-of-Year Diagnostic Test

31. The net of a triangular prism is shown below. What is the surface area of the prism?

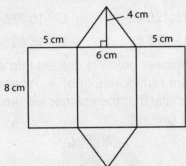

    A   128 cm²   C   176 cm²

    B   152 cm²   D   304 cm²

32. A middle school has 470 students. Regina surveys a random sample of 40 students and finds that 28 have cell phones. How many students at the school are likely to have cell phones?

    A   132 students   C   329 students

    B   188 students   D   338 students

33. Which of the following is the solution to the inequality below?

    $$-5x - 10 < 20$$

    A $x > -6$ C $x < -6$

    B $x > -2$ D $x < -2$

34. Nina operates a dog walking service. She charges a flat fee of $15 plus $5 per hour. Which equation represents this linear relationship?

    A $y = 15x - 5$ C $y = 5x - 15$

    B $y = 15x + 3$ D $y = 5x + 15$

35. To the nearest tenth, what is the area of the figure below? Segment *BF* is a line of symmetry of the pentagon *ABCDE*. Use 3.14 for π.

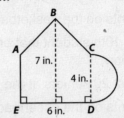

    A   30.3 in²   C   39.3 in²

    B   33.0 in²   D   48.3 in²

36. What is the measure of $\angle BGD$?

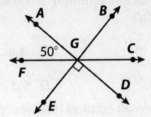

    A   40°   C   90°

    B   50°   D   130°

37. The Masim family's monthly budget is shown in the circle graph below. The family has a current monthly income of $5,000. How much money do they spend on food each month?

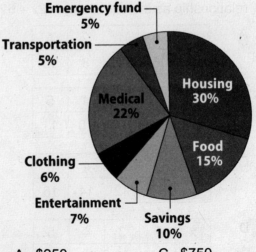

    A $250   C $750

    B $500   D $1,100

Beginning-of-Year Diagnostic Test

38. A box is 30 inches long wide, 16 inches long, and 14 inches high. To the nearest cubic inch, what is the volume of the box?

   A 224 in³   C 480 in³

   B 420 in³   D 6,720 in³

39. A circle has a radius of 7 inches. What is the area of the circle?

   A 21.98 in²   C 153.86 in²

   B 43.96 in²   D 615.44 in²

40. The circle graph shows the results of an employment survey of 800 people. How many of the people surveyed were unemployed?

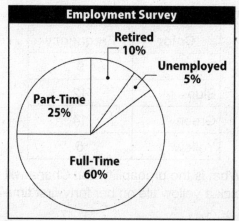

   A 20 people   C 80 people

   B 40 people   D 120 people

41. An equestrian center is surveying riders to determine which type of horse is preferred. Which of the following is a random sampling method?

   A The equestrian center manager surveys the first 50 riders.

   B The equestrian center surveys every tenth rider at the stable.

   C The equestrian center manager surveys 50 of his friends.

   D The equestrian center surveys the 50 best riders.

42. A 16-inch piece of string is 40.64 centimeters long. To the nearest 0.01 a centimeter, how long will a 42-inch piece of ribbon be?

   A 56.64 cm

   B 82.64 cm

   C 106.68 cm

   D 1,706.88 cm

43. One circle has a diameter of 6 inches. A second, larger circle has a diameter that is four times the diameter of the first circle. What is the ratio of the area of the smaller circle to the larger circle?

   A 2:3   C 1:16

   B 1:6.4   D 1:64

Use the box plot for 44–45.

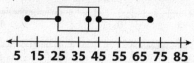

44. What is the median?

   A 10   C 40

   B 25   D 45

45. What is the interquartile range?

   A 10   C 40

   B 20   D 45

Use the figure for 46–47.

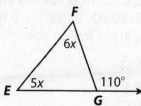

46. What is the measure of ∠FEG?

   A 30°   C 50°

   B 40°   D 70°

Beginning-of-Year Diagnostic Test

47. Which of the following is **not** true?

    A $5x + 6x = 70°$

    B $5x + 6x < 180°$

    C $5x + 6x = 110°$

    D $5x + 6x + 70° = 180°$

48. Which equation represents the data shown in the table below?

Cost (y)	5	9	13	17
Gallon (x)	2	4	6	8

    A $y = 2x + 1$ C $y = 2.5x$

    B $y = 3x - 1$ D $y = 2.5x + 1$

49. Which number line represents the solution to the inequality below?

    $$x - 2 \geq 3$$

    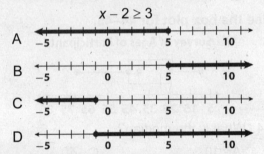

50. Three stores have the same tablet computer on sale. The regular price of the tablet is $150. Store A is offering the tablet on sale at 15% off the regular price. Store B is offering a $25 coupon to be deducted from the regular price. Store C is offering a rebate of $20.00 to purchasers. Store D has the tablet on sale for $120.00. Which store is offering the tablet at the lowest cost?

    A Store A

    B Store B

    C Store C

    D Store D

51. The circumference of a circle is 12π feet. What is the radius of the circle?

    A 3 ft   C 12 ft

    B 6 ft   D 24 ft

52. The Demir family has a monthly budget of $5,500. Mrs. Demir works fulltime and takes home $4,000 each month. Mr. Demir works part-time and brings home earns $16 per hour. How many hours per month must Mr. Demir work at his part-time job to make sure that he and Mrs. Demir have met their monthly budget?

    A 37.5 h   C 93.75 h

    B 75 h   D 125 h

53. Chana has a bag of colored tiles. Without looking, she removes one tile, records the color, and replaces it. She repeats this process 40 times and records the results in the table.

Color	Frequency
Red	9
Blue	12
Green	14
Yellow	5

    What is the probability that Chana will not pick a yellow tile on her forty-first time?

    A $\dfrac{1}{8}$ C $\dfrac{7}{8}$

    B $\dfrac{1}{4}$ D $\dfrac{9}{10}$

54. Mills Middle School has 280 students. A random sample of 30 students were asked how many cars their families have at home. The results are shown in the dot plot below.

    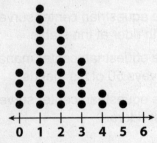

Beginning-of-Year Diagnostic Test

Which of the following is a qualitative statement that is reasonable based on the data?

A   The fewest number of cars at home is 0.

B   Most students have 2 or fewer cars at home.

C   Most students have 3 or more cars at home.

D   The median number of cars at home is 3.

55. Aaron buys 3 ties for $19.95 each, a belt for $23.50, and a pair of boots for $124.95. The sales tax in his city is 5%, To the nearest cent, what is the total cost of Aaron's purchases?

A $176.82   C $218.72

B $197.77   D $304.29

56. The probability of spinning an odd number on a spinner is 62 percent. What is the probability of **not** spinning an odd number?

A   0.28   C   0.48

B   0.38   D   0.62

57. The dot plots below show the number of hours per week that some sixth graders and eighth graders play video games. What is the difference between the mode for sixth graders and the mode for eighth graders?

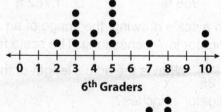

6th Graders

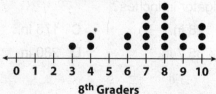

8th Graders

A   3 h   C   8 h

B   5 h   D   13 h

58. A baseball player gets a hit 20% of the times he is at bat. Out of the next 15 times at bat, how many hits can you expect the player to get?

A   2 hits   C   5 hits

B   3 hits   D   12 hits

59. What is the volume of the prism below?

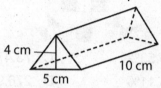

A   100 cm³   C   150 cm³

B   125 cm³   D   200 cm³

60. What is the value of x in the equation below?

$$5x - 35 = 40$$

A   −1   C   −15

B   1   D   15

61. To the nearest hundredth, what is the area of the figure below? Use 3.14 for π.

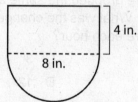

A   57.12 in²   C   200.96 in²

B   128 in²   D   328.96 in²

62. Mike has $75 to spend at a local model car show. The entrance price for the show is $20. At one seller's stand, Mike finds some model cars that he likes that are $7.50 each. What is the maximum number of model cars that Mike can buy at that stand?

A   6 cars   C   8 cars

B   7 cars   D   10 cars

Beginning-of-Year Diagnostic Test

63. A 7-by-7 foot rug is shown below. A coin is tossed onto the rug randomly. What is the probability that the coin will land on an area that is white?

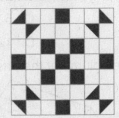

   A 26.53%   C 73.47%

   B 36.11%   D 276.92%

64. On a road map, the distance from Greenmount to Yorktowne is 2 inches. The map scale is 1 in.:25 mi. How many miles is the actual distance between the two cities?

   A 12.5 mi   C 50 mi

   B 25 mi   D 125 mi

65. The temperature in Jukkasjarvi, Sweden, was –3° at 3 P.M. After 6 hours, the temperature dropped to –15°. The temperature dropped the same amount each hour. What was the change in temperature each hour?

   A –2°   C 3°

   B –5°   D 12°

66. The two quadrilaterals below are similar. What is the length of $\overline{EF}$?

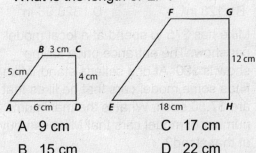

   A 9 cm   C 17 cm

   B 15 cm   D 22 cm

67. The Canadian $2 coin has a diameter of 28 millimeters. To the nearest 0.01 mm, what is the circumference of this coin?

   A 87.92 mm   C 615.44 mm

   B 175.84 mm   D 2,461.76 mm

68. Rinaldo is buying a new truck for $36,000. He is entitled to an 8% rebate. How much will the truck cost after the rebate?

   A $22,800   C $33,120

   B $29,520   D $35,999

69. A bike rental company charges a $10 fee plus $5 per hour. Sofia has $25 to spend. Which inequality could you use to find x, the number of hours Sofia could rent a bike?

   A $10x + 5 > 25$ C $10x + 5 \geq 25$

   B $5x + 10 < 25$ D $5x + 10 \leq 25$

70. To the nearest square meter, what is the area of the figure below?

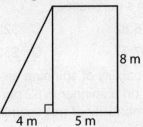

   A 32 m²   C 56 m²

   B 40 m²   D 72 m²

71. The Dead Sea is at an elevation of –1,360 feet. A seabird is flying over the Dead Sea at an elevation of –422 feet. If the bird lands on the Dead Sea, what will be its change in elevation?

   A –1,782 ft   C 938 ft

   B –938 ft   D 1,782 ft

72. On a scale drawing, the image of an alligator is 7 inches long. The scale factor is $\frac{1}{25}$. What is the actual length of the alligator in inches?

   A 28 in.   C 175 in.

   B 35.7 in.   D 280 in.

Beginning-of-Year Diagnostic Test

73. Norfolk Island near Australia has an area of 36 square kilometers. The area of Bermuda is 1.8 times that of Norfolk Island. To the nearest tenth, what is the area of Bermuda?

A 4.5 km²   C 64.8 km²

B 6.5 km²   D 648 km²

74. Becky earned $21,280.08 last year. She earned the same amount each month. To the nearest penny, how much did she earn per month last year?

A $177.33   C $2,103.34

B $1,773.34   D $2,883.39

75. Omar spins both the spinners below. What is the probability that he will land on red and a number less than 5?

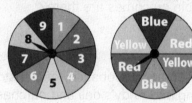

A $\dfrac{1}{64}$ C $\dfrac{4}{27}$

B $\dfrac{3}{32}$ D $\dfrac{5}{27}$

76. Each hour, the temperature rose by $1\dfrac{1}{2}$ degrees. What was the change in temperature in $1\dfrac{1}{2}$ hours?

A $1\dfrac{1}{4}$ degrees   C $2\dfrac{3}{4}$ degrees

B $2\dfrac{1}{4}$ degrees   D 3 degrees

77. One triangle has sides that measure 8 yards, 15 yards, and 17 yards. The side lengths of a second triangle are 48 yards, 90 yards, and 102 yards. What is the constant of proportionality between the first and second triangle?

A $\dfrac{1}{11}$ C 6

B $\dfrac{1}{6}$ D 11

78. A supermarket is having a sale on canned foods. The sale includes 10 cans of beans for $12.50. What is the unit price per can of beans?

A $0.80   C $1.75

B $1.25   D $2.25

79. Beth says the graph below shows last year's temperatures in degrees Celsius.

Which of these could **not** have been one of last year's temperatures?

A −11.3°C   C 7.6°C

B −0.9°C   D 10.3°C

80. A larger circle contains white, striped, and black squares in the same ratio as those shown in the circle below. If the larger circle contains 162 squares, how many of them are black?

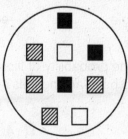

A 36 squares   C 72 squares

B 54 squares   D 126 squares

Beginning-of-Year Diagnostic Test

81. A rectangular prism is 5 meters long, 2 meters wide, and 2 meters high. What is the surface area of this prism in square inches?

    A 20 m^2 C 52 m^2

    B 48 m^2 D 100 m^2

82. Simplify the expression below.

$$-3\left(\frac{1}{6}\right)(2) \div \frac{1}{4}$$

    A −2   C 1

    B −4   D 3

83. Four students put their game scores on the number line below. What is the combined score of students B and D?

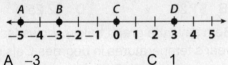

    A −3   C 1

    B 0   D 3

84. Ava wants to leave a 20% tip for the server at a restaurant. Which expression represents the total amount Ava should pay, if m is the price of the meal?

    A $2m$ C $m + 0.2m$

    B $0.2m$ D $m + 20m$

85. A rectangular prism is sliced by a horizontal plane. What is the shape of the cross-section?

    A triangle   C rectangle

    B circle   D trapezoid

86. What is the probability of flipping two coins and both landing tails?

    A 0.25   C 2.5

    B 1.5   D 4

87. Which statement is true about the line segments below?

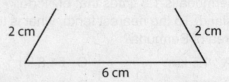

    A They can form a unique triangle.

    B They can form more than one triangle.

    C They cannot form a triangle.

    D It cannot be determined whether they can form a triangle.

88. At a school carnival you pick a ball from two different containers. Each container has red balls and green balls. How many possible outcomes are there?

    A 2   C 6

    B 4   D 8

89. The theoretical probability of a customer walking into Andy's deli and purchasing a sandwich is 6 in 10. Which of the following predictions about Andy's deli is most likely true?

    A The next 6 customers will purchase a sandwich.

    B The next 10 customers will purchase a sandwich.

    C 6 out of the next 100 customers will purchase a sandwich.

    D 12 out of the next 20 customers will purchase a sandwich.

90. Simplify the expression below.

$$2x - 3(y - 2x)$$

    A $8x - 3y$ C $-4x - 3y$

    B $-3y$ D $2x - 3y$

MODULE 1

Adding and Subtracting Integers
Module Quiz: B

1. Georgina works on the 30th floor of an office building. She took the elevator to the cafeteria on the 7th floor. How many floors did she travel?

   A 7   C 30

   B 23   D 37

2. Which of the following expressions has the greatest value?

   A $-3 + -4 - (-2)$ C $-3 + -4 - 2$

   B $-3 - (-4) - (-2)$ D $-3 - (-4) - 2$

3. Which of the following is modeled with the number line below?

   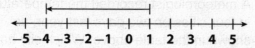

   A $1 + (-4)$ C $1 - (-5)$

   B $1 + (-5)$ D $1 - (-4)$

4. Danielle is playing a game. She started with 10 points. In the first round she lost 20 points. In the second round she won 45 points. Which of the following shows the changes in Danielle's score?

   A $10 - 20 + 45$ C $-10 - 20 + 45$

   B $10 - 20 - 45$ D $-10 - 20 - 45$

5. Which of the following has the same value as $-10 + -3$?

   A $-10 - 3$ C $-3 + 10$

   B $-10 - (-3)$ D $-3 - (-10)$

6. Which of the following is the additive inverse of -3?

   A $-\dfrac{1}{3}$ C $\dfrac{1}{3}$

   B 0   D 3

7. What number can be added to -4 to get a sum of 0?

   A -4 C $\dfrac{1}{4}$

   B 0   D 4

8. Mike deposited $200 into his bank account. He then wrote checks for $20 and $30. Then he deposited $40 dollars more. Which of the following represents the changes in the value of Mike's account?

   A $200 - 20 - 30 + 40$

   B $200 - 20 + 30 + 40$

   C $200 + 20 - 30 - 40$

   D $200 + 20 - 30 + 40$

9. A submarine's elevation is -14 feet relative to sea level. A shark is swimming at an elevation of -56 feet. What is the difference in elevation between the submarine and the shark?

   A 42 ft   C 60 ft

   B 56 ft   D 70 ft

10. The temperature in Montreal was $-8°$C. In New York the temperature was $11°$C. How many degrees warmer was the temperature in New York?

    A 3   C 11

    B 8   D 19

11. What is the value of $-2 + 100 - (-50)$?

    A 48   C 150

    B 148   D 152

12. Danny scored 10 points in the first round of a game. He then lost 20 points in the second round. In the final round he earned 40 points. What was Danny's score at the end of the game?

    A 10   C 30

    B 20   D 40

MODULE 1

Adding and Subtracting Integers

13. Sean, Christian, Anthony, and Mike went to brunch together. Sean paid $30, Christian paid $10, and Anthony paid $20. If the total bill was $75, how much did Mike pay?

_____

14. Jenya deposited $400 into her bank account. A couple of days later she withdrew $50. The next day she deposited $20 more. A day later she withdrew $150.

Write an expression that represents the change in Jenya's account balance.

_____

15. Write an addition or subtraction problem that is modeled by the number line below.

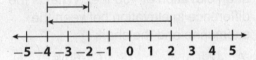

-5 -4 -3 -2 -1 0 1 2 3 4 5

_____

16. Tyrell went to the park to go jogging. The beginning of the running path has an elevation of -2 feet. The highest elevation on the jogging path is 14 feet. What is the difference in elevation between the highest point and the beginning of the path?

_____

17. The value of $x + y$ is negative, and x is a positive integer. What must be true about y? Explain.

_____

18. What is the value of $-3 - (-10) - 8$?

_____

19.

Temperature in Four Cities

City	Temperature on Day 1 (°C)	Temperature on Day 2 (°C)
A	-5°	-1°
B	-12°	-8°
C	-11°	-2°
D	-3°	5°

A meteorologist recorded the temperature in four cities on two days last year, as shown in the table above. Which city had the greatest increase in temperature between the two days?

_____

20. The value of $x - y$ is negative, and x and y are both positive. What can you conclude about the values of x and y?

_____

21. Luisa claims that when she subtracts two negative integers, the result is always positive. Is she correct? Explain.

_____

22. -2, -1, -1, 0, -1, 1, -2, …

Find the next 3 numbers in the sequence above. Describe the pattern.

_____

_____

MODULE 1 — Adding and Subtracting Integers

Module Quiz: D

1. Charles works on the 12th floor of an office building. He went to lunch at the cafeteria on the 4th floor. How many floors down did Charles go when he took the elevator to lunch?

   A 8

   B 12

   C 16

2. Which of the following expressions has the greatest value?

   A $-2 - 3$

   B $-2 - (-3)$

   C $2 - (-3)$

3. Which of the following is modeled with the number line below?

   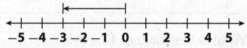

   A $0 - 3$

   B $0 + 3$

   C $-3 + -3$

4. Maritza is playing a game. She started with -10 points. In the first round she won 20 points. Which of the following shows the change in Martiza's score?

   A $-10 + 20$

   B $-10 - 20$

   C $10 + 20$

5. Which of the following has the same value as $-10 + -3$?

   A -13

   B -7

   C 13

6. What number can be added to -2 to get a sum of 0?

   A -2

   B 0

   C 2

7. Tyler deposited $300 into his bank account. He then wrote a check for $150. Which of the following represents the changes in the value of Tyler's account?

   A $300 - 150$

   B $300 + 150$

   C $150 - 300$

8. A diver's elevation is -5 feet relative to sea level. A school of fish is swimming at an elevation of -12 feet. What is the difference in elevation between the diver and the school of fish?

   A 7 feet

   B 10 feet

   C 17 feet

9. The temperature in Vancouver was $-6°C$. In Austin the temperature was $10°C$. How many degrees warmer was the temperature in Austin?

   A 4

   B 10

   C 16

10. What is the value of $-2 + 9$?

    A -7

    B 7

    C 11

11. What is the sum of -15 and -125?

    A -140

    B -115

    C 140

MODULE
1

Adding and Subtracting Integers

12. If Jon paid $20 towards the $80 cost of a sweater, how much does he still owe?

_____

13. Ryan deposited $100 into his bank account. Later in the week he withdrew $75 from the account.

Write an expression that represents the change in Ryan's account balance.

_____

14. Write an addition or subtraction problem that is modeled by the number line below.

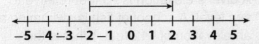

_____

15. Tamika went hiking with her friends. The beginning of the hiking path has an elevation of –1 feet. The highest elevation on the hiking path is 100 feet. What is the difference in the two elevations?

_____

16. The value of x is negative. What must be true about $10 - x$? Explain.

_____

17. What is the value of $-3 - (-8)$?

_____

18. What is the sum of –10 and –25?

_____

19. What is the value of $-11 - (-10)$?

_____

20.

Temperature in Four Cities

City	Temperature on Day 1 (°C)	Temperature on Day 2 (°C)
A	–5°	–1°
B	–12°	–8°
C	–11°	–2°
D	–3°	5°

By how many degrees did the temperature increase in City A from Day 1 to Day 2?

_____

21. What is the value of $12 + (-5)$?

_____

22. What number can be added to 9 to get a result of 0?

_____

23. –2, –4, –6, –8, …

Find the next 3 numbers in the sequence above. Describe the pattern.

_____

_____

24. –2, 0, –2, 0, …

Find the next 3 numbers in the sequence above. Describe the pattern.

_____

_____

MODULE 2

Multiplying and Dividing Integers
Module Quiz: B

1. A shopper uses a department-store gift card to pay for 3 sweaters priced at $27 each. What is the change in the value of the gift card?

   A −$81

   B −$27

   C −$24

   D $81

2. When her elevator was out of service, Debi walked down 21 flights of stairs. She stopped to rest after every 3 flights. How many times did Debi stop to rest?

   A −63

   B −31

   C 18

   D 7

3. Last week, Clay wrote 4 checks for $20 each from his checking account, withdrew another $30, and finally made a deposit of $96. What was the change in the balance of his account over the week?

   A −$46

   B −$14

   C $14

   D $46

4. Which expression would be evaluated as a positive number?

   A $\dfrac{(-3)(-4)}{(-6)}$

   B $\dfrac{(3)(-4)}{(6)}$

   C $\dfrac{(-3)(4)}{(6)}$

   D $\dfrac{(-3)(4)}{(-6)}$

5. Philip played a board game, and he drew 4 straight cards that read, "Go back 8 spaces." What is the change in Philip's position on the game board?

   A −136 spaces

   B −32 spaces

   C 46 spaces

   D 104 spaces

6. Manuel played an arcade game that cost 25 tokens per game. In six games, Manuel won 0 tokens, 10 tokens, 50 tokens, 0 tokens, 5 tokens, and 10 tokens. What is the change in the number of tokens Manuel has?

   A −85

   B −75

   C 75

   D 90

7. The low temperature for 5 days was −5°, −7°, −2°, 2°, and −3°. What was the average low temperature for those days?

   A −4°   C −2°

   B −3°   D −1°

8. A football team was given 3 penalties for 15 yards each and 2 penalties for 5 yards each. What was the total change in their field position from these penalties?

   A −85 yd

   B −75 yd

   C −55 yd

   D −20 yd

9. Amy bought 3 pounds of lemons at $2 per pound, a box of rice for $4, and 7 frozen dinners for $3 each. What is the change in the amount of money she has?

   A −$39

   B −$31

   C −$9

   D $31

MODULE 2 Multiplying and Dividing Integers

10. In 1924, the temperature in Fairfield, Montana, dropped from 63 degrees to −21 degrees in 12 hours. What was the average hourly change in temperature?

_____

11. a. Write a multiplication expression containing at least 3 terms that has a negative answer.

   _____

   b. How could you change this expression so that it has a positive answer?

   _____

12. Doug lost his measuring tape, so he had to estimate the length of a board he had to cut. He cut off 2 inches, but the board was still too long. He did this 4 times. After the fourth cut, the board was the right length. Write and find the value of an expression to find the change in the length of the board.

_____

13. The panda at the zoo became ill and lost 4 pounds every week for 5 weeks. In the sixth week, she began to feel better and gained 3 pounds. Write and find the value of an expression for the change in the panda's weight over these 6 weeks.

_____

14. Over 8 days, the price of a share of XYZ Company stock fell $72. On the ninth day, the price rose $4, but on the tenth day, it fell $12. Write and find the value of an expression for the average change in the price of the stock for these 10 days.

_____

15. The Salton Trough has an elevation of 69 meters below sea level. The Dead Sea Depression is almost 6 times deeper. Write and find the value of an expression for the approximate elevation of the Dead Sea Depression.

_____

16. Race car driver Mario won 3 races and earned 75 points for each win. During the fourth race, he had deductions of 55 points, 104 points, and 85 points, but earned 3 points for finishing. Write and find the value of an expression for how many points he has now.

_____

17. Deepak bought a new video game. While he learned how to play, he played 6 games and had a combined score of −1,044 points. Write and find the value of an expression for the average number of points he lost in the first 6 games.

_____

18. For 8 days of very hot weather, the water level in a lake dropped 3 inches per day. On the ninth day, storms raised the level 6 inches. Write and find the value of an expression for the change in the water level of the lake during these 9 days.

_____

19. Marla has a piece of fabric. She cuts off 8 inches and makes a bow for each of the dogs she grooms. Today she groomed 12 dogs. Write and find the value of an expression for the change in the length of the fabric.

_____

MODULE 2

Multiplying and Dividing Integers
Module Quiz: D

1. During a football game, the visiting team was given 4 penalties for 15 yards each. What was the change in the visiting team's field position due to these penalties?

   A −90 yd

   B −80 yd

   C −60 yd

2. In 1943, the temperature in Rapid City, South Dakota, fell about 45 degrees in 5 minutes. What was the average drop in temperature per minute?

   A −40°

   B −9°

   C 50°

3. Louisa used a gift card to pay for 3 meals at a vegetarian restaurant. Each meal cost $7. By how much has the value of the gift card changed?

   A −$21

   B −$10

   C −$7

4. Fred withdrew $20 from his checking account on Monday. He withdrew another $20 from the account on Friday. Which expression shows how the balance of Fred's checking account has changed?

   A 20 + 20

   B 2 − 20

   C 2(−20)

5. Which expression has the value of −2?

   A $\dfrac{(3)(4)}{(6)}$

   B $\dfrac{(-3)(4)}{(6)}$

   C $\dfrac{(-3)(-4)}{(6)}$

6. Adam was learning to play a new board game. He spun the spinner 5 times, and each time it landed on "Go back 4 spaces." How did the position of Adam's game piece change over these 5 spins?

   A −20 spaces

   B −4 spaces

   C 20 spaces

7. Mrs. Jones got a new freezer. She plugged it in, and it began to get cold. The temperature inside the freezer dropped 12 degrees every hour for 6 hours. What was the change in the temperature in the freezer over those 6 hours?

   A −104°

   B −96°

   C −72°

8. The price of 1 share of stock fell $4 every day for 3 straight days. How did the price of the stock change over these 3 days?

   A −$36

   B −$12

   C −$7

9. Every time Megan takes a sip of water, the level of the water in her glass goes down 1 inch. She takes 3 sips. How much did the level of the water in Megan's glass change?

   A −6 in.

   B −3 in.

   C −1 in.

MODULE 2

Multiplying and Dividing Integers

10. A cold front moved in last weekend. In 8 hours overnight, the temperature outside dropped 24 degrees. What was the average temperature change for each hour?

_____

11. How could you change the expression $(-8)(-5)(-3)$ so that the product is positive?

_____

12. A mine equipment room is 40 meters below the surface of the ground. The work area of the mine is 5 times deeper. What is the elevation of the work area?

_____

13. While he was playing a video game, Zach would lose 12 points every time his character's hat was blown off. In one game, he lost 9 hats this way. How did the number of points Zach had change from all the lost hats?

_____

14. Shondra bought a spool of ribbon. She uses 30 inches of the ribbon to decorate each gift box. She decorated 7 gift boxes in all. What number describes the change in the length of ribbon on the spool?

_____

15. What number could be added to the product of $(-7)(-6)$ so that the sum is equal to 27?

_____

16. Li bought his dog Spot a huge bone. Spot chews 4 inches off the bone every day. What number describes the change in the length of the bone after 3 days?

_____

17. Paul is tearing down a long brick wall. He can tear down 5 feet of the wall every day. What will be the change in the length of the wall after 5 days?

_____

18. What is the last operation to be performed when finding the value of this expression?

$5 + (-8) \div (-3) + (-9)(-6)$

_____

19. Demond bought 4 bags of popcorn at the movie theater. Each bag cost $2. What is the change in the amount of money Demond has?

_____

20. What number could be added to the quotient of $(-48) \div (-8)$ so that the sum is equal to -17?

_____

21. At a restaurant, 8 plates are accidently broken every day for a week. What number represents the change in the number of plates the restaurant has?

_____

MODULE 3

Rational Numbers

Module Quiz: B

1. What is the product of –1.24 and 4.25?

   A –5.27   C 3.01

   B –3.01   D 5.49

2. Ben walked $\frac{2}{5}$ mile. Tonya walked $\frac{1}{4}$ mile. What fraction of a mile did they walk in total?

   A $\frac{1}{10}$ mi   C $\frac{7}{20}$ mi

   B $\frac{1}{3}$ mi   D $\frac{13}{20}$ mi

3. What is $6\frac{3}{8}$ written as a decimal?

   A 5.625   C 6.38

   B 6.375   D 8.6

4. Tameka built $\frac{1}{2}$ of a shed on Monday and $\frac{2}{5}$ of the shed on Tuesday. Tameka finished building the shed on Wednesday. What fraction of the shed did she build on Wednesday?

   A $\frac{1}{10}$ C $\frac{3}{7}$

   B $\frac{2}{5}$ D $\frac{9}{10}$

5. A box of cereal contains 23.4 ounces. It costs $5.49. What is the cost, to the nearest cent, of the cereal per ounce?

   A $0.23   C $4.26

   B $2.35   D $28.89

6. Syeda had $80.45 in her bank account on Monday. She deposited $20.50 on Tuesday. She then withdrew $37.25 on Wednesday. How much did Syeda have left in her account on Thursday?

   A $63.70   C $97.20

   B $80.45   D $138.20

7. A ribbon is $12\frac{3}{8}$ feet long. Into how many $\frac{3}{4}$-foot pieces can it be cut?

   A 9   C 15

   B 10   D 16

8. Alexander purchased a computer on sale. The original price was $1,200. The sale price was $\frac{5}{6}$ of the original price. How much did Alexander pay for the computer?

   A $900   C $1,144

   B $1,000   D $1,440

9. On a certain day the temperature in New York City was –4°C and the temperature in Austin was 10°C. How many degrees lower was the temperature in New York City?

   A 6°C   C 10°C

   B 7°C   D 14°C

10. A deep-sea diver descended from a rock that is 45 feet below sea level to a coral reef that is 88 feet below sea level. How far did the diver descend from the rock to the coral reef?

    A 43 feet   C 88 feet

    B 67 feet   D 123 feet

MODULE 3 **Rational Numbers**

11. Jared bought a cell phone for $42. Juanita spent $1\frac{1}{2}$ times as much. How much did she spend?

_____

12. What is the value of $-\frac{2}{5} \div \frac{3}{4}$?

_____

13. What is the product of -2.5 and 8.77?

_____

14. Jeunesse earned $725 dollars by working 5 days in a week. What is the average amount that she earned per day?

_____

15. Ben paid $900 for a sofa. The price of the sofa Juana purchased was $\frac{2}{3}$ the price that Ben paid. How much did Juana pay for her sofa?

_____

16. Anna made 400 quarts of lemonade. She poured the lemonade into containers. Each container holds $\frac{4}{7}$ of a quart. How many containers did Anna use?

_____

17. Sanin went to the store to buy groceries. He bought a box of cereal for $5.29, a gallon of milk for $2.49, and a quart of juice for $3.79. He paid the cashier with a $20 bill. How much change did Sanin receive?

_____

18. What is the value of $-6 + -3 - (-18)$?

_____

19. Mara finished $\frac{1}{5}$ of her assignment on Saturday and $\frac{3}{8}$ of her assignment on Sunday. What fraction of her assignment did she complete on Saturday and Sunday?

_____

20. Jean-Claude equally shared a box of chocolates with two of his friends. The box weighed $\frac{9}{5}$ pounds. How many pounds of chocolate did each person receive?

_____

21. The Smith family took a car trip. They traveled $\frac{1}{2}$ the distance from San Antonio to Austin on Monday and $\frac{3}{12}$ the distance on Tuesday. What fraction of the distance between San Antonio and Austin did the Smith family travel on Monday and Tuesday?

_____

22. Amory ate $\frac{1}{4}$ of a box of cereal. Blaine ate $\frac{2}{9}$ of the same box. What fraction of the box of cereal did they eat together?

_____

MODULE 3

Rational Numbers
Module Quiz: D

1. Dillon read $\frac{1}{5}$ of a book on Monday and $\frac{2}{5}$ of the book on Tuesday. What fraction of the book did he read on Monday and Tuesday?

   A $\frac{2}{25}$

   B $\frac{3}{10}$

   C $\frac{3}{5}$

2. Which of the following is equal to $-2 - 5$?

   A -7

   B -3

   C 7

3. Which of the following fractions is equal to a terminating decimal?

   A $\frac{1}{3}$

   B $\frac{2}{5}$

   C $\frac{7}{9}$

4. A box of granola contains 16.8 ounces. It costs $5.19. What is the cost, to the nearest cent, of the granola per ounce?

   A $0.12

   B $0.31

   C $3.24

5. What is the value of $(-0.8)(4.0)$?

   A -4.8

   B -3.2

   C 3.2

6. A computer was on sale for $\frac{2}{3}$ of the original price. If the original price was $900, what was the sale price?

   A $300

   B $600

   C $1,350

7. What is the value of $-2.4 \div 1.5$?

   A -1.6

   B -0.9

   C 1.6

8. Tyrell was late for class 3 times in the month of June. Each time he was late he missed $5\frac{1}{2}$ minutes of class time. What is the total amount of class time Tyrell missed in the month of June?

   A $8\frac{1}{2}$ minutes

   B 15 minutes

   C $16\frac{1}{2}$ minutes

9. Ben's family went on a car trip. They stopped for gas 4 times. Each time they stopped they spent an average of 15 minutes at the gas station. On their trip, about how much time did Ben's family spend stopping for gas?

   A 45 minutes

   B 60 minutes

   C 75 minutes

10. Pietro sailed his sailboat 1,260 yards in 30 minutes. What is the average number of yards he traveled per minute?

    A 21

    B 30

    C 42

MODULE 3 **Rational Numbers**

11. Max played a video game in which he scored 1,440 points after 12 rounds. What is the average number of points he won per round?

_____

12. Martin wants to buy 4 plastic figures that cost $17 each. How much money does he need to save to purchase the figures?

_____

13. What is the number $5\frac{2}{7}$ written as an improper fraction?

_____

14. Profits at Carla's Craft shop decreased by $1,015 in one week. On average, by how much did profits decrease each day?

_____

15. Simran waited $3\frac{1}{2}$ hours for her car to get repaired. What is $3\frac{1}{2}$ written as a decimal?

_____

16. During a sale, all video games are $10 off. Rebecca used a coupon to get an additional $15 off her purchase. If the original price of a video game was $60, how much did Rebecca pay?

_____

17. What is the product of −0.2 and −6.8?

_____

18. Tyra's purse weighs $2\frac{1}{4}$ pounds. What is the weight of her purse expressed as a decimal?

_____

19. Manny drove 45 miles in 0.75 hours. What was the average rate that he drove in miles per hour?

_____

20. Kai went on a bike ride. Every time he stops to drink water, his bike ride takes 3 minutes longer. If he stops to drink water six times, how much longer does his bike ride take?

_____

21. Damian's computer repair shop earned $2,500 in income last week. Expenses were $3,750. What was Damian's profit or loss for the week?

_____

22. Karen bought a handbag for $55. Agnes spent 1.5 times as much on hers. How much did Agnes spend?

_____

23. Wally purchased a desk that was on sale for $\frac{2}{3}$ of the original price. If the original price was $450, what was the price that Wally paid?

_____

24. What is the value of $-1\frac{2}{3} \div 1\frac{7}{18}$ expressed as a mixed number?

_____

MODULE 4

Rates and Proportionality

Module Quiz: B

1. A machine paints 340 toy boats in 45 minutes. Which expression equals the unit rate per hour?

   A $\dfrac{\frac{3}{4}}{340}$

   B $\dfrac{45}{340}$

   C $\dfrac{340}{\frac{3}{4}}$

   D $\dfrac{340}{45}$

2. Which speed is the fastest?

   A 18 feet in 20 minutes

   B 90 feet in 2.5 hours

   C 20 yards in 1.5 hours

   D $3\frac{2}{3}$ yards in 15 minutes

3. What is the unit price for a piece of cheese if 1.24 pounds costs $11.25?

   A $0.11 per lb

   B $9.07 per lb

   C $12.49 per lb

   D $13.95 per lb

4. Which table shows a constant rate of change?

   A
Days	6	12	18
Earnings ($)	225	450	750

   B
Days	6	12	18
Earnings ($)	225	500	750

   C
Days	6	12	20
Earnings ($)	225	450	675

   D
Days	6	12	20
Earnings ($)	225	450	750

5. A student spends the same amount each week for bus fare. In 5 weeks, he spends $115. Which equation shows this relationship? Let x = number of weeks.

   A $y = 3.22x$

   B $y = 5x$

   C $y = 23x$

   D $y = 115x$

Use the graph for 6–7.

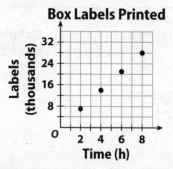

Box Labels Printed

6. Draw a line through the points. Why does this line show a proportional relationship?

   A It is not curved.

   B It is a vertical line.

   C It connects all the dots.

   D It goes through the origin.

7. What is the constant of proportionality for the relationship on the graph?

   A 3.5   C 8

   B 7   D 28

8. If a is an integer, when is $\dfrac{a}{b}$ always equal to an integer?

   A $b = 0$ C $b > 1$

   B $b < 1$ D $b = 1$ or -1

MODULE 4

Rates and Proportionality

9. Complete the table for an object that goes $\frac{3}{4}$ miles in 6 minutes.

Distance (mi)	$\frac{3}{4}$	$1\frac{1}{2}$	$2\frac{1}{4}$
Time (h)	$\frac{1}{10}$		

10. If a person bikes 2.4 miles in 10 minutes, how far can he bike in 1.5 hours?

_____

11. Explain how to simplify this complex fraction. Interpret the meaning of the result.

$$\frac{330 \text{ pages}}{\frac{3}{4} \text{ hour}}$$

_____

_____

12. Find k, the constant of proportionality, for the data in this table. Then write an equation for the relationship.

x	25	50	75	100
y	160	320	480	640

_____

13. Create a table that shows a proportional relationship. Do not use an integer for the constant of proportionality.

Number of Cookies	6	12	20
Cost ($)			

14. A car traveled at a constant speed of 45 miles per hour. Make a graph to show how the distance traveled in miles is related to the time in hours.

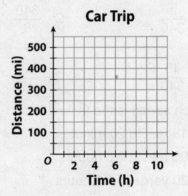

Car Trip

Use the graph for 15–16.

Savings Account

15. What equation shows the line through the data points on the graph?

_____

16. Write an equation for someone saving more money per week. Add a line to the graph for this equation.

_____

_____

17. An object travels $\frac{4}{5}$ miles in one-half hour. What is its speed?

_____

MODULE 4

Rates and Proportionality

Module Quiz: D

1. A student used the complex fraction below to find a unit rate.

$$\frac{340 \text{ pages}}{\frac{3}{4} \text{ hour}}$$

Which quotient equals the fraction?

A $\frac{3}{4} \div 340$

B $\frac{4}{3} \div 340$

C $340 \div \frac{3}{4}$

2. Which speed is the fastest?

A 4 miles in $\frac{1}{3}$ hour

B $\frac{1}{3}$ mile in 4 hours

C $\frac{1}{2}$ mile in 3 hours

3. If 4.5 pounds of cherries cost $10, what is the unit price?

A $0.22 per pound

B $0.45 per pound

C $2.22 per pound

4. Which table shows a constant rate of change?

A

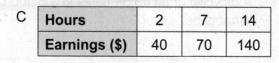

Hours	2	7	14
Earnings ($)	40	60	80

B

Hours	2	7	14
Earnings ($)	40	140	280

C

Hours	2	7	14
Earnings ($)	40	70	140

5. A student studies the same amount of time each day for a test. In 4 days, she studied 60 minutes. Which equation shows this relationship? Let x = the number of days.

A $y = 4x$

B $y = 15x$

C $y = 60x$

Use the graph for 6–7.

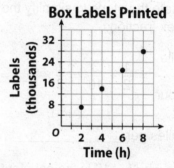

Box Labels Printed

6. Draw a line through the points. How many labels are printed in 10 hours?

A 24

B 35

C 40

7. Which term best describes the relationship between time and number of labels printed?

A double

B decreasing

C proportional

8. Which of these is **not** an integer?

A $\frac{6}{3}$ C $\frac{6}{2}$

B $\frac{3}{6}$

MODULE 4 Rates and Proportionality

9. Complete the table for an object that goes 20 miles in $\frac{1}{4}$ hour.

Distance (mi)	20		
Time (h)	$\frac{1}{4}$	$\frac{1}{2}$	$\frac{3}{4}$

10. If a person walks 2.4 miles in 1.5 hours, how far can he walk in 3 hours?

_____

11. Complete the steps to simplify the complex fraction.

$$\frac{\frac{1}{2} \text{ mile}}{\frac{3}{10} \text{ hour}} = \frac{1}{2} \div \frac{3}{10} = \frac{1}{2} \times \underline{\quad} =$$

____ miles per _____

12. Explain why $k = 10$ is the constant of proportionality for this table.

x	25	50	75	100
y	250	500	750	1,000

_____

_____

13. Create a table that shows a proportional relationship. Then use your table to find the cost of 10 pounds.

Number of Pounds	1	2	3
Cost ($)			

cost for 10 pounds = _____

14. Some hikers had an average speed of 2 miles per hour. Draw a graph to show how the distance is related to the time. Plot at least 4 points and draw a line through the points.

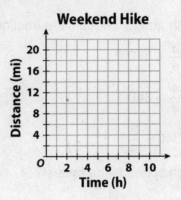

Weekend Hike

Use the graph for 15–16.

Savings Account

15. Draw a line through the points. How much money is saved in 5 weeks?

_____

16. Write two ordered pairs to show that the equation $y = 15x$ represents the data.

_____

17. A bicyclist goes 43.54 miles in 3.5 hours. What is her speed?

_____

MODULE 5 Proportions and Percent

Module Quiz: B

Use the table for 1–2.

Sales Tax in Cities	
River City	3%
Springfield	4.1%
Thompsonville	2.9%
Union City	3.2%

1. Liz wants to buy a shirt for $25. How much will Liz's shirt cost in Springfield rounded up to the nearest cent?

   A $25.50

   B $26.00

   C $26.03

   D $36.66

2. How much more will her shirt cost in Union City than in River City?

   A $0.01

   B $0.05

   C $0.10

   D $25.80

3. A town's population went from 25,800 to 42,600 in 15 years. What was the percent of change?

   A 35%

   B 39.4%

   C 61%

   D 65.1%

4. A gym's membership in 2010 was 8,700. Now, it is 6,400. Which expression equals the percent of change?

   A $6,400 \div 8,700$

   B $8,700 - 6,400$

   C $(8,700 - 6,400) \div 8,700$

   D $(8,700 - 6,400) \div 6,400$

5. A store marks up sporting goods 27%. Which expression equals the retail price of an item with an original cost of p dollars?

   A $p \times 0.27$

   C $p \times 0.73$

   B $p \div 0.27$

   D $p \times 1.27$

6. A toy store marks down every toy by 15% in January. How much does a toy cost during January? Use p for the price in December.

   A $0.15p$

   C $0.85p$

   B $0.75p$

   D $1.15p$

7. A market buys mixed nuts at $12.50 per pound. They want to make a 22% profit. What should they charge for the retail price?

   A $2.75/lb

   C $15.25/lb

   B $9.75/lb

   D $34.50/lb

8. A student spends $48 on school supplies at a store where the sales tax is 7%. What is the total cost of the supplies?

   A $3.36

   C $51.36

   B $33.60

   D $55.00

9. What is the annual interest for a principal of $3,500 at a simple annual interest rate of 2.3%?

   A $80.50

   C $3,580.50

   B $805.00

   D $4,305.00

10. Which expression does this number line show?

   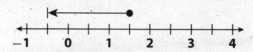

   A $-0.5 - 1.5$

   C $1.5 - 2$

   B $1.5 - (-0.5)$

   D $1.5 + 2$

MODULE 5 | **Proportions and Percent**

11. What is one way to find the total cost of a jacket for $55.80 with a sales tax of 2.7%?

_____

12. What is another way to find the total cost of a jacket for $55.80 with a sales tax of 2.7%?

_____

13. The price of a $250 coat increased 7% last year. The coat is now on sale for one-half off. What is the sale price?

_____

Use the table for 14–15.

Population Changes

Town	2000	2010
Lakeside	51,342	45,863
Centerville	37,065	26,102
Riverview	41,726	63,017

14. Find the percent of change to the nearest tenth of a percent for Centerville.

_____

15. Which town had the greatest percent of change? What was the percent?

_____

16. A clerk is marking up merchandise 34%. The original price of an item is $455. What will be the retail price?

_____

17. At the end of the summer, a store marks down all the outdoor furniture 18%. A family bought 4 chairs in June at $35 each, then 2 more chairs when they went on sale. How much did all 6 chairs cost?

_____

18. A shopper paid $51.93 including tax for an item marked $48.99. What would she pay for another item marked $75?

_____

19. An amount of $8,000 is invested at a simple interest rate of 1.5%. What is the total amount after 3 years?

_____

20. A restaurant bill before tax is $15.50. If the sales tax is 8% and a 15% tip is added, what is the total cost of the meal?

_____

21. Find k, the constant of proportionality, for the data in this table. Then write an equation for the relationship.

x	10	15	20	25
y	65	97.5	130	162.5

_____

MODULE 5

Proportions and Percent

Module Quiz: D

Use the table for 1–2.

Sales Tax in Cities	
City A	3%
City B	4.1%
City C	2.9%
City D	3.2%

1. Tom wants to buy a sweater for $30. In which city will it be least expensive?

   A City A

   B City B

   C City C

2. How much will Tom's $30 sweater cost in City B?

   A $30.90

   B $31.23

   C $30.87

3. The population of a town was 25,000 people. Then 3,200 people moved away. What was the percent of decrease?

   A 12.8%

   B 21.8%

   C 78.1%

4. In 3 years, a gym's membership went up from 6,400 to 8,400. Which expression shows how to find the percent of increase?

   A 2,000 ÷ 8,400

   B 2,000 ÷ 6,400

   C 6,400 ÷ 2,000

5. What is a markup?

   A a percent of increase

   B the retail price of an item

   C a discount on an original price

6. A toy store marks down every toy by 15% in January. How much does a toy cost during January?

   A 15% of the original price

   B 85% of the original price

   C 15% more than the original price

7. A market buys mixed nuts at $15 per pound. They want to make a 20% profit. What would you pay for 1 pound of nuts?

   A $3

   B $15

   C $18

8. The price of a graphing calculator is $80. The sales tax is 7%. What is the total cost of the calculator?

   A $5.60

   B $85.60

   C $87.00

9. An amount of $4,000 is invested. The interest rate is 2%. What is the amount earned in one year?

   A $80

   B $420

   C $800

10. Which subtraction problem is shown on the number line?

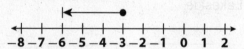

   A −6 − (−3)

   B −3 − 3

   C −3 − (−6)

MODULE 5   **Proportions and Percent**

11. What is one way to find the total cost of a pair of shoes for $57 with a sales tax of 2%?

_____

12. What is another way to find the total cost of a pair of shoes for $57 with a sales tax of 2%?

_____

_____

_____

13. Last year a winter coat cost $175. This year the price increased 15%. What is the new price?

_____

Use the table for 14–15.

Population Changes

Town	2000	2010
Lakeside	51,300	45,800
Centerville	37,000	26,100
Riverview	41,700	63,000

14. Find the percent of decrease for Lakeside.

_____

15. One town had an increase of population. Find the percent of increase.

_____

16. Some students are raising money by selling greeting cards. They buy the cards for $3 a box and then mark up the price by 30%. For how much do they sell each box of cards?

_____

17. A store is going out of business. Everything is marked down 40%. How much do you pay now for an item that used to cost $150?

_____

18. A shopper paid $432 for an item marked $400. What was the percent of the sales tax?

_____

19. How much interest is earned in one year on $5,000 at an interest rate of 3%?

_____

20. A restaurant bill before tax is $15.50. How much is a 15% tip for this bill?

_____

21. Write an equation that shows the relationship in this table.

Time in Hours (x)	1	2	3	4
Distance in Miles (y)	50	100	150	200

$y =$ _____

MODULE 6 — Expressions and Equations

Module Quiz: B

1. Which of the following is the solution to the equation below?

$$x - 1.4 = 0.6$$

   A 0.8   C 1.2

   B 1.0   D 2.0

2. Lani opened a savings account with $450. She saves $225 per month. Which equation shows how much money Lani has in her account after m months?

   A $y = -\dfrac{450}{225}m$

   B $y = 450m + 225m$

   C $y = 450 + 225m$

   D $y = 225 + 450m$

3. What is the value of y that satisfies the equation below?

$$\dfrac{y}{3} = 12$$

   A 3   C 36

   B 4   D 63

4. Kimmy earns a $200 commission on all sales plus a base salary of $30,000. Her total income last year was $80,000. Which equation can be used to calculate the number of Kimmy's sales?

   A $30{,}000 + 200x = 80{,}000$

   B $30{,}000 - 200x = 80{,}000$

   C $200 + 30{,}000x = 80{,}000$

   D $80{,}000 + 200x = 30{,}000$

5. Rashida owns a bike rental company. She charges an initial fee of $10 for each rental and an hourly rate of $4. Which of the equations below shows the amount y that Rashida charges for a bike rental that lasts x hours?

   A $y = 10 + 4x$ C $y = 4 + 10x$

   B $y = 10 - 4x$ D $y = 4 - 10x$

6. Which of the following uses the Distributive Property?

   A $0.4 \times (2a - 0.3b) = 0.4 + (2a - 0.3b)$

   B $0.4 \times (2a - 0.3b) = \dfrac{(2a - 0.3b)}{0.4}$

   C $0.4 \times (2a - 0.3b) = 0.8a - 0.12b$

   D $0.4 \times (2a - 0.3b) = 0.8a \times 0.12b$

7. The chess club has 50 members. They want to raise $680 for a trip to a competition. The school will give $130. How much must each member pay?

   A $5   C $11

   B $10   D $550

8. Which of the following ratios is **not** equivalent to 1:4?

   A $\dfrac{1}{2}$ C $\dfrac{3}{12}$

   B $\dfrac{2}{8}$ D $\dfrac{4}{16}$

9. Which of the following values does **not** satisfy the inequality $-2x - 6 \le 1$?

   A -4 C -2

   B -3 D -1

10. Alexa started a race with a 50-meter head start. She ran at a rate of 6.25 meters per second. After how many seconds was Alexa 200 meters past the starting line?

   A 20   C 32

   B 24   D 40

11. Jamie has 6 quarters and some dimes in his pocket. The total value of the coins is $4.50. How many dimes does he have in his pocket?

   A 10   C 30

   B 20   D 40

MODULE 6

Expressions and Equations

12. Massimo has $90 in the bank. Every time he rides the bus he spends $2.50. Write and solve an equation that Massimo can use to see how many times he can ride the bus.

_____

13. Timani bought a video game console and some games for $350. The video game console cost $200. Each game cost $25. How many games did Timani purchase?

_____

14. Allison bought some shirts for her clothing store for $15 each. She received $50 off her entire purchase and spent a total of $400. How many shirts did Allison purchase for her store?

_____

15. Jane has 6 more than half the number of pairs of shoes that Mercedes has. Write an expression for this.

_____

16. Write a word phrase for $0.3x + 5$.

_____

17. Kelly has 4 dimes and some nickels. The total value of her coins is $2.25. Write an equation for this.

_____

18. Solve for x.

$$0.25x = 10$$

_____

19. Paco solved the equation $-3x - 5 = 1$. His work is shown below.

   Step 1: $-3x - 5 = 1$

   Step 2: $-3x = 6$

   Step 3: $x = 2$

   Where did Paco make an error in his calculation? Explain.

_____

20. Oswaldo earns a salary of $2,500 per month plus an 8% commission on all of his sales. He wants to earn $5,400 next month. Write an equation that shows what his total sales s must be in order for Oswaldo to reach his goal.

_____

21. Wallace has a $50 bill. Pizza pies cost $12.25 each. If p represents the number of pizzas he buys, write an expression for the change he receives.

_____

22. Juma earns $12.50 for each newspaper subscription he sells. He also earns a $50 base salary each week. If he wants to earn $400 next week, how many newspaper subscriptions does he need to sell? Write an equation and solve.

_____

MODULE 6 Expressions and Equations
Module Quiz: D

1. What is the solution to the equation below?

$$0.5x = 6$$

   A 3

   B 12

   C 60

2. Alyson opened a savings account with $100. She saves $50 per month. Which of the following equations can be used to find how much money she has in her account after *x* months?

   A $100 + 50x = y$

   B $50 + 100x = y$

   C $600 + 50x = y$

3. What is the value of *y* that satisfies the equation below?

$$\frac{y}{2} = 9$$

   A 4.5

   B 9

   C 18

4. Ed earns a $100 commission on each computer he sells plus a base salary of $50,000. His total income last year was $75,000. Which equation can be used to find how many computers Ed sold last year?

   A $50,000 + 100x = 75,000$

   B $50,000 - 100x = 75,000$

   C $75,000 + 100x = 50,000$

5. Jason pays a $100 installation fee and a $40 monthly service charge for his telephone. Which equation shows the amount that Jason pays for *x* months of telephone service?

   A $y = 40 + 100x$

   B $y = 100 + 40x$

   C $y = 100 - 40x$

6. There are 60 members in the school glee club. The glee club needs to raise $5,000 for a trip to a national competition. The school agreed to contribute $1,000 toward the trip. Which of the equations below shows the amount of money that each glee club member needs to raise to help pay for the trip?

   A $60x + 1,000 = 5,000$

   B $60x + 5,000 = 1,000$

   C $1,000x + 60 = 5,000$

7. Which of the following shows the simplification of $0.5 \times (4a + 6b)$ using the Distributive Property?

   A $2a + 3b$

   B $3a + 2b$

   C $4.5a + 6.5b$

8. Which of the following ratios is equivalent to 1:2?

   A $\frac{2}{4}$

   B $\frac{3}{5}$

   C $\frac{4}{6}$

9. Which of the following values does **not** satisfy the equation $x - 2 = 3.5$?

   A $5\frac{1}{2}$

   B 5.5

   C 1.5

10. Colton's Gym charges an initiation fee of $40 plus a monthly fee of $50. Which of the equations below shows the cost *c* of joining the gym for *m* months?

   A $c = 50 + 40m$

   B $c = 40 + 50m$

   C $c = 40 - 50m$

MODULE 6	**Expressions and Equations**

11. Beth has $108.50 in her bank account. She buys x shirts for $5.50 each. Write and solve an equation Beth can use to find how many shirts she can buy.

_____

12. What is the solution to the equation below?

$$-\frac{2}{3}x = 20$$

_____

13. Morgan used the equation below to find the number of mini netbooks she could purchase to fit her budget.

$$87.5x = 350$$

How many mini netbooks can Morgan buy?

_____

14. Guillermo bought some reams of paper for $5 each and a $200 printer. He spent a total of $450. Write and solve an equation to find the number of reams of paper Guillermo purchased.

_____

15. Tallulah has 40 dimes and some nickels. The total value of her change is $5.00. How many nickels does Tallulah have?

_____

16. Dexter wrote the equation below to find the number of hours he would need to work at $10 an hour to save $300.

$$10x + 160 = 300$$

According to this equation, how much money did Dexter already have saved before he started working?

_____

17. Nadya solved the equation $4x - 4 = 20$. Her work is shown below.

Step 1: $4x - 4 = 20$
Step 2: $4x = 16$
Step 3: $x = 4$

Where did Nadya make an error in her calculation? Explain.

_____

18. Consuela earns a salary of $40,000 per year plus a commission of $1,000 for each car she sells. Write and solve an equation that shows the number of cars Consuela must sell in order to make $60,000 in one year.

_____

19. What is the absolute value of –200?

_____

20. Shilpa earned 100 points in the first round of a game. She earned 20 points in each of the following rounds of the game. She ended the game with 400 points. Write and solve an equation to find the number of rounds Shilpa played.

_____

21. Benjamin rides the train to work. He spends $2.75 per ride. His monthly budget for riding the train is $80. Write an equation that shows the number of times, n, Benjamin can ride the train each month.

_____

22. Solve the equation below for y.

$$\frac{5}{6}y = 12$$

_____

MODULE 7	**Inequalities**

Module Quiz: B

1. What is a value of y that satisfies the inequality below?

$$\frac{y}{3} \le 12$$

A 42   C 38

B 39   D 36

2. Which of the following is a solution to the inequality below?

$$2x > 6$$

A –3   C 3

B 2   D 5

3. Parvinder wants to save $500 for a trip. Which inequality shows the least amount she must save each month for 6 months to accomplish this?

A $6x \le 500$ C $6x \ge 500$

B $6x < 500$ D $x \ge 500 + 6$

4. TJ earns a 20% commission on all sales plus a base salary of $40,000. His total income last year was more than $70,000. Which inequality can be used to calculate the minimum number of TJ's sales?

A $40,000 + 0.2x \ge 70,000$

B $40,000 - 0.2x \ge 70,000$

C $0.2 + 40,000x \ge 70,000$

D $70,000 + 0.2x \ge 40,000$

5. Tony wants to buy a ticket for $15.75. He has $9.25. How much must he earn to buy the ticket?

A at least $6.00

B less than $6.00

C at least $6.50

D at least $7.00

6. Peggy wants to run 5 miles in less than 60 minutes. What inequality shows what her rate should be?

A 1 mi < 60 min   C 1 mi < 12 min

B 3 mi < 60 min   D 2 mi < 30 min

7. There are 125 members in the school marching band. The band wants to raise $25,000 for a trip to a national competition. The school agreed to contribute $5,000 towards the trip. Which inequality shows the amount of money that each band member should raise?

A $125x + 25,000 \ge 5,000$

B $125x + 5,000 \ge 25,000$

C $5,000x + 125 \ge 25,000$

D $5,000x + 25,000 \ge 125$

8. Which of the following is the solution to the inequality $-2x - 4 \le 11$?

A $x \le -\dfrac{15}{2}$ C $x \ge -\dfrac{15}{2}$

B $x \le -\dfrac{7}{2}$ D $x \ge -\dfrac{7}{2}$

9. Which of the following ratios is **not** equivalent to 2:10?

A $\dfrac{1}{5}$ C $\dfrac{4}{20}$

B $\dfrac{2}{5}$ D $\dfrac{6}{30}$

10. Which of the following values does **not** satisfy the inequality $-2x - 6 \le 1$?

A –4   C –2

B –3   D –1

11. Michele needs 30 ounces of pecans to bake some pies. Pecans are sold in 4-ounce packages. Which inequality could be used to find the least number of packages of pecans she has to buy?

A $\dfrac{30}{x} \le 4$

B $\dfrac{4}{x} \le 30$

C $4x \ge 30$

D $x \le 30 - 4$

Name ______________________ Date ______________ Class ______________

MODULE 7

Inequalities

12. Solve the inequality. Show your work.

$$\frac{x}{6} \leq 1$$

Use the inequality for 13 and 14.

$$x + 8 \geq 5$$

13. Solve the inequality. Show your work.

14. Graph the solution on the number line.

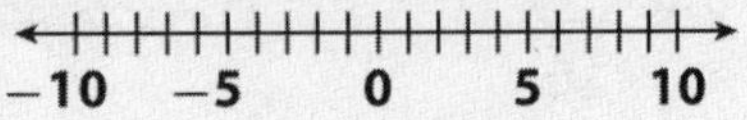

Use the inequalities for 15–17.

$$-3x > 9$$

$$3x > -9$$

15. Explain the difference between the two inequalities. How does this affect your method of solution?

16. Solve the first inequality and graph its solution on the number line.

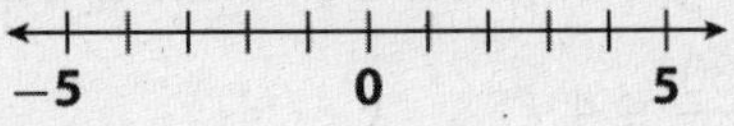

17. Solve the second inequality and graph its solution on the number line.

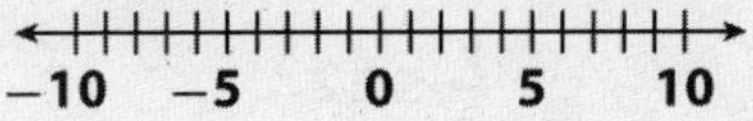

18. Raja solved the inequality $-3x - 5 \leq 1$. His work is shown below.

Step 1: $-3x - 5 \leq 1$

Step 2: $-3x \leq 6$

Step 3: $x \leq -2$

Where did Raja make an error in his calculation? Explain.

19. Joaquim earns a salary of $4,000 per month plus a 6% commission on all of his sales. He wants to earn at least $7,000 next month. Write an inequality that shows what his total sales s must be in order for Joaquim to reach his goal.

20. Every month, the bank withdraws $15 from Betsy's checking account as a service fee. Betsy has budgeted $75 for the next few service fees. For how many months will the service fee be covered? Write and solve an inequality to find the solution. Show your work.

MODULE 7

Inequalities

Module Quiz: D

1. Which is a solution to the inequality below?

$$x > 6$$

   A −6

   B 6

   C 7

2. Tito opened a savings account with $100. He saves $25 per month. Which of the inequalities below can be used to find the least number of months it will take Tito to have $700 saved?

   A $100 + 25x \geq 700$

   B $25 + 100x \geq 700$

   C $700 + 25x \geq 100$

3. What is a value of y that satisfies the inequality below?

$$\frac{y}{2} > 9$$

   A 9

   B 18

   C 19

4. Ed earns a $100 commission on each computer he sells plus a base salary of $50,000. His total income last year was $75,000. Which equation can be used to find how many computers Ed sold last year?

   A $50,000 + 100x = 75,000$

   B $50,000 - 100x = 75,000$

   C $75,000 + 100x = 50,000$

5. Demarcus has at least $8 more than his older sister. His older sister has $4. Which of the following inequalities could be used to find how much money, m, Demarcus has?

   A $m > 8 + 4$

   B $8 - m < 4$

   C $8m > 4$

6. There are 60 members in the school glee club. The glee club needs to raise at least $5,000 for a trip to a national competition. The school agreed to contribute $1,000 toward the trip. Which of the inequalities below shows the amount of money that each glee club member needs to raise to help pay for the trip?

   A $60x + 1,000 \geq 5,000$

   B $60x + 5,000 \geq 1,000$

   C $1,000x + 60 \geq 5,000$

7. Which of the following is the solution to the inequality below?

$$2x - 4 \leq 12$$

   A $x \leq 8$

   B $x \leq 12$

   C $x \leq 16$

8. Which of the following ratios is equivalent to 1:2?

   A $\frac{2}{4}$

   B $\frac{3}{5}$

   C $\frac{4}{6}$

9. Which of the following values does **not** satisfy the inequality $x - 2 \leq 3$?

   A 3

   B 5

   C 7

10. For which of the following inequalities is $x \geq 4$ a solution?

   A $x + 3 \geq 1$

   B $3x \geq 1$

   C $x - 3 \geq 1$

MODULE 7 | **Inequalities**

11. Beth has $300 in her bank account. She buys *x* shirts for $20 each. What is an inequality Beth can use to find how many shirts she can buy and still have more than $100 in her account?

_____

12. What is a solution to the inequality below?

$$-x + 5 < 20$$

_____

13. Luz used the inequality below to find the maximum number of tablet computers she could purchase to fit her budget.

$$70x < 350$$

What is the greatest number of tablet computers that Luz can buy?

_____

Use the inequality for 14–16.

$$x - 4 \leq 3$$

14. Explain how you would solve the inequality.

_____

_____

15. Solve the inequality. Show your work.

_____

_____

_____

16. Graph the solution on the number line.

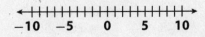

17. Kahal solved the inequality $4x - 4 > 20$. His work is shown below.

Step 1: $4x - 4 > 20$

Step 2: $4x > 16$

Step 3: $x > 4$

Where did Kahal make an error in his calculation? Explain.

_____

_____

18. Fill in the blanks to complete the special rule for inequalities.

If you _____ or

_____ both sides

of an inequality by the same

_____ number,

you must _____ the

inequality symbol for the statement to

still be _____.

19. What is the absolute value of −200?

_____

Use the inequalities for 20–22.

$$x \leq 3$$

$$x < 3$$

20. What is the difference between the two inequalities? Explain.

_____

_____

21. Graph the first equality.

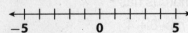

22. Graph the second equality.

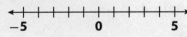

MODULE 8 Modeling Geometric Figures
Module Quiz: B

Use the figure for 1–2.

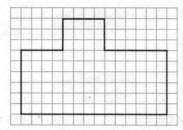

1. The figure shows a scale drawing of a room, and each square stands for 1 square foot. What is the area of the room in square yards?

   A $10\frac{2}{3}$ C 96

   B 32   D 126

2. Now let the figure show a scale drawing of a park with the largest dimension equal to 63 meters. What is the scale?

   A 1 unit : 3.11 m   C 1 unit : 7 m

   B 1 unit : 4.5 m   D 1 unit : 10.5 m

3. Two sides of a triangle measure 25 cm and 35 cm. Which of the following could be the measure of the third side?

   A 3 cm   C 8 cm

   B 6 cm   D 11 cm

4. A triangle has two sides that measure 5 cm and 7 cm. Which of the following CANNOT be the measure of the third side?

   A 3 cm   C 7 cm

   B 5 cm   D 12 cm

5. A store sells towels for 25% off the regular price. The regular price of a beach towel is $24.50. Which expression represents the sale price?

   A 0.25x   C 1.25x

   B 0.75x   D 1.75x

6. The right rectangular prism below has a square base.

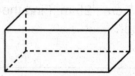

The following could be the shape of a cross section of the prism EXCEPT:

   A rectangle   C parallelogram

   B circle   D square

7. Which of the following can form a cross section?

   A a point and a triangle

   B a plane and a cone

   C a circle and a square

   D a line and a point

Use the diagram for 8–9.

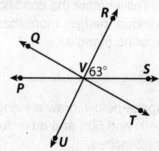

8. What is the measure of ∠PVU?

   A 15°   C 63°

   B 33°   D 117°

9. Which describes the relationship between ∠QVP and ∠PVU?

   A adjacent angles

   B complementary angles

   C supplementary angles

   D vertical angles

10. Joey cut a 10.5-foot length of rope into 6 pieces of equal length. How long was each piece of rope?

   A 0.25 ft   C 2.5 ft

   B 1.75 ft   D 6 ft

MODULE 8

Modeling Geometric Figures

11. A scale drawing for a rectangular parking lot measures 6.8 cm by 12.3 cm. The scale is 5 cm : 25 m. Find the area of the parking lot.

_____

12. The scale drawing below is the base of an office building. The scale of the drawing is 1 unit : 6 feet.

Redraw the scale drawing using a scale of 1 unit : 4 yards. Use the grid above.

13. A triangle has angles measuring 30° and 90°. The length of the included side is 6 cm. Tell whether the conditions form a unique triangle, more than one triangle, or no triangle.

_____

14. In the space below, draw a triangle with angles 40° and 50°, and an included side length of 2 inches.

15. Patricia bought a new swimsuit that cost $35. Sales tax is 7.5%. How much did Patricia pay, including sales tax?

_____

Use the figure for 16–17.

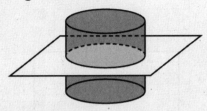

16. Describe the cross section of the cylinder by naming its shape.

_____

17. Is it possible for the cylinder to have a cross section in the shape of a rectangle? Explain.

_____

_____

Use the diagram for 18–19.

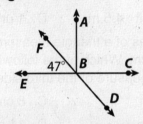

18. What is the measure of ∠EBD?

_____

19. What is the relationship between ∠ABF and ∠ABD?

_____

20. Deborah has $6\frac{1}{2}$ pounds of cherries. She wants to divide them into plastic bags with $\frac{1}{4}$ pound of cherries in each bag. Find the number of plastic bags she will need.

_____

MODULE 8

Modeling Geometric Figures

Module Quiz: D

Use the figure for 1–2.

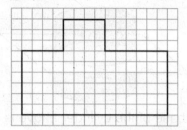

1. The figure shows a scale drawing of a room. Each square shows 1 square foot. What is the perimeter of the room?

   A 14 ft

   B 46 ft

   C 96 ft^2

2. Now let the figure show a scale drawing of a park. The scale is 1 unit : 25 meters. What is the horizontal distance across the actual park?

   A 14 m

   B 225 m

   C 350 m

3. Two sides of a triangle measure 20 cm and 30 cm. Which of the following could be the measure of the third side?

   A 3 cm

   B 6 cm

   C 11 cm

4. A triangle has two sides that measure 5 cm and 7 cm. Which of the following CANNOT be the measure of the third side?

   A 3 cm

   B 10 cm

   C 17 cm

5. A store sells baskets for 50% off the retail price. The retail price of a basket is $24. What is the sale price?

   A $10

   B $12

   C $20

6. The right rectangular prism below has a square base.

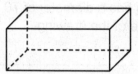

The following could be the shape of a cross section of the prism EXCEPT:

   A rectangle

   B circle

   C square

7. A cross section can be formed by the intersection of a plane and which of the following?

   A point

   B cone

   C line

Use the diagram for 8–9.

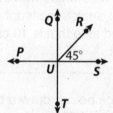

8. What is the measure of ∠RUP?

   A 45°

   B 90°

   C 135°

9. Which describes the relationship between ∠TUP and ∠TUS?

   A adjacent angles

   B complementary angles

   C vertical angles

10. Nikita cut a 10.5-foot length of rope into 2 pieces of equal length. How long was each piece of rope?

   A 2.5 ft

   B 5.25 ft

   C 10 ft

MODULE
8

Modeling Geometric Figures

11. A scale drawing shows a circular fountain with a diameter of 7 units. The actual fountain has a diameter of 70 feet. Find the scale of the drawing.

_____

12. A parking lot has the shape of a rectangle. A scale drawing for the parking lot measures 6 cm by 20 cm.

The scale is 1 cm : 15 m.
Find the area of the parking lot.

_____

13. Tell whether you can make a unique triangle or no triangle with these conditions: angles measuring 45° and 90° an included side that is 10 cm.

_____

14. In the space below, draw a triangle with angles 60° and 60°, and an included side length of 2 inches.

15. Olga bought a new skirt that cost $20. Sales tax is 5%. How much did Olga pay, including sales tax?

_____

Use the figure for 16–17.

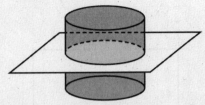

16. The base of the cylinder above is a circle. Name the shape of the cross section of the cylinder.

_____

17. Sketch the cross section in the space below.

Use the diagram for 18–19.

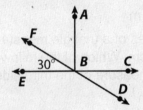

18. What is the measure of ∠FBC?

_____

19. What is the relationship between ∠ABC and ∠CBD?

_____

20. Akram has 3 pounds of cherries. He wants to divide them into plastic bags with $\frac{1}{2}$ pound of cherries in each bag. Find the number of plastic bags he will need.

_____

MODULE 9 **Circumference, Area, and Volume**
Module Quiz: B

1. What is the circumference of the circle below?

18 m

A 36 m   C 113 m

B 56.5 m   D 324 m

2. What is the area of the circle below?

27 m

A 42.4 m²   C 572.3 m²

B 84.8 m²   D 729.1 m²

3. What is the area of the figure below?

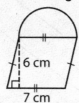

6 cm

7 cm

A 42 cm²   C 80.5 cm²

B 61.2 cm²   D 118.9 cm²

4. Karen bought 5.5 pounds of bananas for $0.40 per pound. How much did she pay for the bananas?

A $2.20   C $4.50

B $3.40   D $5.70

5. What is the surface area of the rectangular prism below?

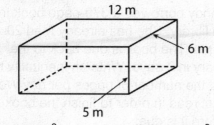

12 m

6 m

5 m

A 60 m²   C 162 m²

B 72 m²   D 324 m²

6. What is the volume of the triangular prism below?

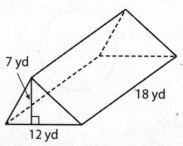

7 yd

18 yd

12 yd

A 42 yd³   C 756 yd³

B 84 yd³   D 1,512 yd³

Use the figure for 7–8.

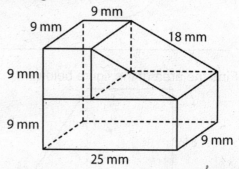

9 mm

9 mm

18 mm

9 mm

9 mm

9 mm

25 mm

7. What is the surface area of the figure above?

A 785 mm²   C 1,692 mm²

B 1,467 mm²   D 1,854 mm²

8. What is the volume of the figure above?

A 929 mm³   C 2,025 mm³

B 1,296 mm³   D 3,402 mm³

9. Henry joined an art class that charges $125 for the cost of supplies, plus $25 per class. Henry wants to spend no more than $500 on art classes. Which inequality can be solved to find the number of classes Henry can take?

A $25x + 125 < 500$

B $125x - 25 > 500$

C $25x \geq 625$

D $125x + 25 \leq 500$

MODULE 9 **Circumference, Area, and Volume**

10. Find the circumference of the circle below.

52 yd

_____

11. Find the area of the circle below.

13 ft

_____

12. Find the area of the figure below.

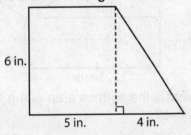

6 in.

5 in.   4 in.

_____

13. A half cup of milk has 4 grams of protein. Find the number of grams of protein in $2\frac{1}{4}$ cups of milk.

_____

14. Find the surface area of the triangular prism below.

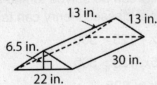

13 in.   13 in.

6.5 in.

30 in.

22 in.

_____

15. Find the volume of the trapezoidal prism below.

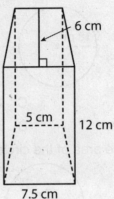

6 cm

5 cm   12 cm

7.5 cm

_____

Use the figure for 16–17.

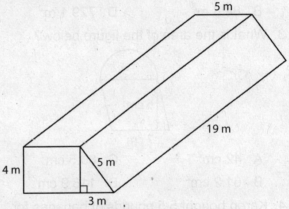

5 m

19 m

4 m   5 m

3 m

16. Find the surface area of the figure.

_____

17. Find the volume of the figure.

_____

18. Wendy borrowed a 370-page book from the library. She has already read 20 pages. The book is due back to the library in 7 days. Write an inequality to find the number of pages per day Wendy must read in order to finish the book before it is due.

_____

MODULE 9 **Circumference, Area, and Volume**
Module Quiz: D

1. What is the circumference of the circle below? Use the formula $C = 2\pi r$.

5 m

A 5π m

B 10π m

C 20π m

2. What is the area of the circle below? Use the formula $A = \pi r^2$.

3 m

A 3π m^2

B 6π m^2

C 9π m^2

3. What is the area of the figure below?

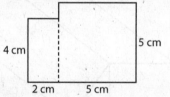

5 cm

4 cm

2 cm   5 cm

A 25 cm^2

B 33 cm^2

C 65 cm^2

4. What is 5×0.5?

A 2.5

B 3.5

C 5.5

5. What is the surface area of the rectangular prism below?

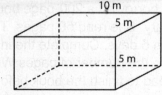

10 m

5 m

5 m

A 250 m^2

B 200 m^2

C 175 m^2

6. What is the volume of the triangular prism below? (*Hint:* The formula for the area of a triangle is $A = \dfrac{1}{2}bh$.)

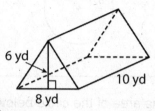

6 yd   10 yd   8 yd

A 60 yd^3

B 240 yd^3

C 480 yd^3

Use the figure for 7–8.

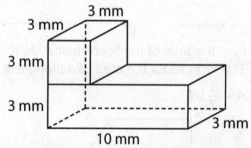

3 mm   3 mm   3 mm   3 mm   3 mm   3 mm   10 mm

7. What is the surface area of the figure above?

A 138 mm^2

B 174 mm^2

C 192 mm^2

8. What is the volume of the figure above?

A 27 mm^3

B 90 mm^3

C 117 mm^3

9. Henry takes an art class that charges $100 for supplies, plus $20 per class. Henry wants to spend less than $500 on art classes. Which inequality can be solved to find x, the number of classes Henry can take?

A $20x + 100 < 500$

B $100x + 20 > 500$

C $20x \geq 600$

MODULE 9 **Circumference, Area, and Volume**

10. Find the circumference of the circle below. Use the formula $C = 2\pi r$.

8 ft

_____

11. Find the area of the circle below. Use the formula $A = \pi r^2$.

10 ft

_____

12. Find the area of the figure below. *Hint:* The formula for the area of a triangle is $A = \frac{1}{2}bh$.

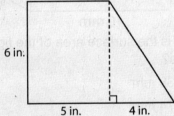

6 in.

5 in.   4 in.

_____

13. A cup of milk has 8 grams of protein. How much protein is in 2.5 cups of milk?

_____

14. Find the surface area of the triangular prism below.

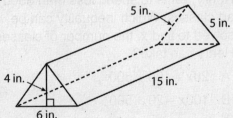

5 in.

5 in.

4 in.

15 in.

6 in.

_____

15. Find the volume of the trapezoidal prism below. *Hint:* The formula for the area of a trapezoid is $A = \frac{1}{2}(b_1 + b_2)h$.

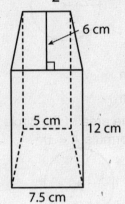

6 cm

5 cm   12 cm

7.5 cm

_____

Use the figure for 16–17.

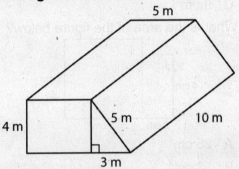

5 m

4 m

5 m   10 m

3 m

16. Find the surface area of the figure. Be sure to include the areas of all the sides that you cannot see.

_____

17. Find the volume of the figure.

_____

18. Wendy borrowed a 200-page book from the library. She read 50 pages. The book is due in 5 days. Complete the inequality to find x, the number of pages Wendy must read to finish the book before it is due.

$5x \geq 200 -$ _____

MODULE 10

Random Samples and Populations
Module Quiz: B

1. Which of these statements best describes a biased sample?

   A It is very small.

   B It is not randomly chosen.

   C It results in incorrect predictions.

   D It does not accurately represent the population.

2. In a survey about new bike paths, which group is least likely to be a biased sample?

   A randomly chosen voters

   B randomly chosen drivers

   C randomly chosen dog-walkers

   D randomly chosen gym members

Use the dot plot for 3–5.

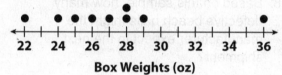

Box Weights (oz)

A shipping manager weighed a random sample from a shipment of 90 boxes and made the dot plot above.

3. Which range of weights has the greatest number of boxes?

   A 22–25   C 28–30

   B 25–29   D 30–36

4. Which box plot shows the same data as the dot plot?

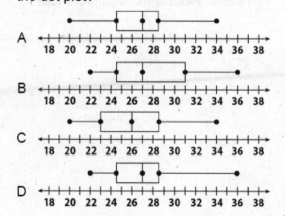

5. Use the data to estimate the weight of all 90 boxes.

   A 2,000 oz   C 3,000 oz

   B 2,500 oz   D 3,500 oz

6. A town has 35,000 registered voters. A random sample of 500 voters finds that 125 are in favor of a new dog park. How many are likely to vote for the dog park?

   A 25   C 2,625

   B 125   D 8,750

7. Which could be the shape of a cross section of a cone?

   A triangle   C pentagon

   B rectangle   D square

Use the information below for 8–9.

A baker produces 500 loaves a day. On Monday, 50 loaves did not meet quality standards. The baker generates a random sample to simulate 10 loaves to inspect on Tuesday. The integers 1 to 50 represent sub-standard loaves.

| 351 | 207 | 148 | 428 | 272 |
| 121 | 47 | 205 | 56 | 4 |

8. Based on this sample, how many loaves will not meet quality standards on Tuesday?

   A 2   C 100

   B 20   D 150

9. What is the difference between the number of sub-standard loaves produced on Monday and the number predicted to be sub-standard on Tuesday?

   A 10   C 100

   B 50   D 200

10. A circle has a diameter of 50 meters. What is its circumference?

    A 50 m   C 314 m

    B 157 m   D 625 m

MODULE 10

Random Samples and Populations

11. A principal wants to find out if her school needs more bike racks. A survey is taken of 30 students who ride the bus. Why might the sample be biased? Describe a sample that is more representative of the entire school.

_____

_____

_____

Use the data set for 12–16.

Children's Ages
7, 4, 7, 7, 2, 10, 12, 8, 7, 4

The data set shows the ages of a random sample of children under 14 who live in an apartment building.

12. Make a dot plot to display the data.

13. Make a box plot to display the data.

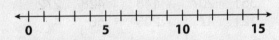

14. What is the age range and the most common age?

_____

15. What is the median age?

_____

16. Is a child in this building whose age is under 14 more likely to be younger than 7 or older than 7?

17. Name two possible shapes that could be the cross section of a rectangular prism.

_____

_____

Use the information below for 18–19.

In a shipment of 2,000 beach balls, 150 are defective. The manufacturer generates a random sample to simulate 20 beach balls to inspect in the next shipment. The integers 1 to 150 represent defective beach balls.

42	1701	638	397	113
1243	912	380	769	1312
76	547	721	56	4
1411	1766	677	201	1840

18. Based on this sample, how many defective beach balls might the manufacturer expect in the next shipment?

_____

19. What is the difference between the number of defective beach balls in the actual shipment and the number predicted in the next shipment?

_____

20. A round swimming pool has a radius of 12 feet. What is its circumference?

_____

MODULE 10 **Random Samples and Populations**
Module Quiz: D

1. In a sample for a survey, each person has the same chance of being chosen. What kind of sample is it?

   A biased

   B random

   C population

2. A survey is taken to find out if people in a town want a new bike path. Which is the **best** group to sample?

   A randomly chosen dog-walkers

   B randomly chosen gym member

   C randomly chosen shoppers at a mall

3. There are 90 boxes to be shipped. The shipping clerk takes a sample of 9 boxes to estimate the total weight.
   The dot plot below shows the weights of the sample.

   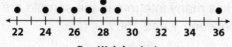

   Box Weights (oz)

   What is the median weight in the sample?

   A 26 oz

   B 27 oz

   C 28 oz

4. The box plot shows the same data as the dot plot above.

   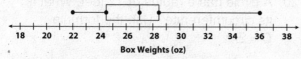

   Box Weights (oz)

   What is the interquartile range?

   A 22-36 oz

   B 27 oz

   C 24.4-28.5 oz

5. Study the box plot in Exercise 4. Use the median to estimate the total weight of all 90 boxes in the shipment.

   A 2,000 oz

   B 2,500 oz

   C 3,500 oz

6. A small town has about 5,000 people. A random sample of 100 people finds that 25 are in favor of a new park. Estimate the total number out of 5,000 who are in favor of the park.

   A 250 people

   B 1,250 people

   C 2,500 people

7. Which could be the shape of a cross section of a cube?

   A square

   B oval

   C circle

Use the information below for 8–9.

On Monday, a baker made 500 loaves of bread and 50 were burned. The baker uses a random sample to simulate 10 loaves to inspect on Tuesday. The integers 1 to 50 represent burned loaves.

| 351 | 207 | 148 | 428 | 272 |
| 121 | 47 | 205 | 56 | 4 |

8. How many integers in the sample are between 1 and 50?

   A 1

   B 2

   C 4

9. What percentage of loaves are predicted to turn out burned on Tuesday?

   A 10%

   B 20%

   C 80%

10. A circle has a radius of 25 meters. What is its circumference? Use the formula $C = 2\pi r$.

   A 50 m

   B 157 m

   C 314 m

MODULE 10 **Random Samples and Populations**

11. A school principal wants to find out if his school needs more bike racks. A survey is taken of 30 students who ride their bikes to school. Why might the sample be biased?

_____

_____

Use the data set for 12–16.

Children's Ages
7, 4, 7, 7, 2, 10, 12, 8, 7, 4

The data set shows the ages of 10 children.

12. On the number line below, make a dot plot to display the data.

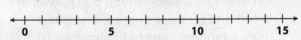

13. What is the most common age of the children in this group?

_____

14. What is the age range?

_____

15. The box plot below shows the same data as the data set above.

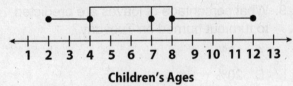

Children's Ages

What is the median age?

_____

16. Is a child in this group more likely to be older than 8 or younger than 8?

_____

17. Name a shape that could be the cross section of a cone.

_____

Use the information below for 18–19.

In a shipment of 2,000 beach balls, 150 are defective. The beach ball company uses a random sample to simulate 20 beach balls to inspect in the next shipment.
The integers 1 to 150 represent defective beach balls.

42	1701	638	397	113
1243	912	380	769	1312
76	547	721	56	4
1411	1766	677	201	1840

18. How many integers in the sample are between 1 and 150?

_____

19. What percentage of beach balls are predicted to be defective in the next shipment?

_____

20. A circle has a radius of 12 feet. What is its circumference? Use the formula $C = 2\pi r$.

_____

MODULE 11

Analyzing and Comparing Data

Module Quiz: B

Use the dot plots for 1 and 2.

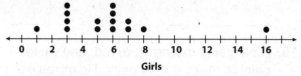

Girls

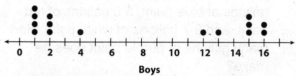

Boys

The dot plots compare the number of raffle tickets sold by boys and girls during a school fundraiser.

1. Which plot has an outlier?

   A Girls

   B Boys

   C both plots

   D neither plot

2. What is the difference between the medians for the two data sets?

   A 0 tickets   C 4 tickets

   B 2 tickets   D 6 tickets

Use the box plots for 3 and 4.

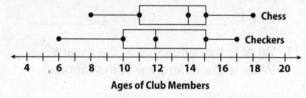

Ages of Club Members

3. What is the interquartile range for the Checkers Club?

   A 4   C 10

   B 5   D 11

4. Which data set shows a greater spread?

   A Chess Club

   B Checkers Club

   C They have the same spread.

   D You cannot tell from the box plots.

5. Kiana is making a recipe. She pours $3\frac{1}{3}$ cups of flour into a bowl. Then she adds $1\frac{1}{4}$ cups of nuts. What is the total amount of ingredients in the bowl?

   A $2\frac{1}{6}$ cups   C $4\frac{7}{12}$ cups

   B $2\frac{3}{4}$ cups   D $5\frac{1}{12}$ cups

Use the information below for 6 and 7.

Statistical measures are shown below for the number of hours per week spent doing homework by the students in two classes.

Class 1: Mean number of hours spent doing homework = 20, mean absolute deviation = 2

Class 2: Mean number of hours spent doing homework = 24, mean absolute deviation = 2

6. What is the difference between the means for the two data sets?

   A 2   C 6

   B 4   D 8

7. Which statement about the data is true?

   A The difference of the means is equal to the mean absolute deviation.

   B The difference of the means is 1.5 times the mean absolute deviation.

   C The difference of the means is 2 times the mean absolute deviation.

   D The difference of the means is 4 times the mean absolute deviation.

8. What is $11\frac{4}{5}$ written as a decimal?

   A 11.4   C 11.8

   B 11.5   D 11.9

MODULE 11

Analyzing and Comparing Data

Use the dot plots for 9–11.

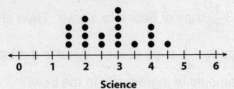

Science

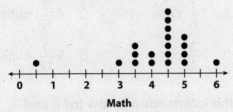

Math

The dot plots show the number of hours students in two classes studied.

9. What percent of each class studied less than 4 hours?

Science: _____ Math: _____

10. Find the medians.

Science: _____ Math: _____

11. Compare the centers and spreads.

_____

_____

Use the box plots for 12–14.

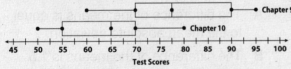

Test Scores

12. Compare the medians.

_____

_____

13. Compare the spreads.

ranges: _____

interquartile ranges: _____

14. Write a conclusion.

_____

15. A painter is mixing blue, red, and white paint to make purple paint. He mixes 6.2 gallons of blue paint, 5.8 gallons of red paint, and 9.7 gallons of white paint. How many gallons of purple paint does he make?

_____

Average monthly temperatures for two cities are shown in the tables below. Use the data below for 16 and 17.

City 1
65, 68, 63, 55, 59, 78, 70, 75, 72, 75, 71, 68

City 2
75, 67, 55, 57, 65, 61, 65, 69, 62, 60, 68, 67

16. Calculate the means to the nearest whole degree.

City 1: _____ City 2: _____

17. What is the difference in the means? What is the difference of the ranges?

_____

18. What is $5\frac{2}{8}$ written as a decimal?

_____

MODULE
11

Analyzing and Comparing Data
Module Quiz: D

Use the dot plots for 1 and 2.

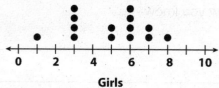

Girls

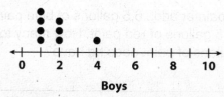

Boys

The two dot plots compare ages of girls and boys in a pottery class.

1. Which group has a greater range?

   A Girls

   B Boys

   C The ranges are the same.

2. Which group has a greater median?

   A Girls

   B Boys

   C The medians are the same.

Use the box plots for 3 and 4.

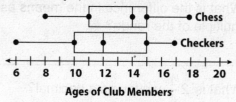

Ages of Club Members

3. Which group has a greater range?

   A Chess

   B Checkers

   C The ranges are the same.

4. Which group has a greater median?

   A Chess

   B Checkers

   C The medians are the same.

5. What is $3\frac{1}{3} + \frac{1}{3}$?

   A $1\frac{1}{3}$

   B $2\frac{2}{3}$

   C $3\frac{2}{3}$

Use the information below for 6 and 7.

Data was collected on hours per week spent doing homework by the students in two classes. Here are statistics on the data:

Class 1:
mean = 20
range = 9

Class 2:
mean = 23
range = 9

6. What is the difference between the means of Class 1 and Class 2?

   A 0

   B 3

   C 9

7. The range is how many more times than the difference of the means?

   A 1

   B 2

   C 3

8. What is $11\frac{1}{2}$ written as a decimal?

   A 11.2

   B 11.25

   C 11.5

MODULE
11   **Analyzing and Comparing Data**

The dot plots show hours some students studied. Use the dot plots for 9–11.

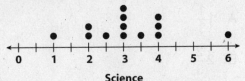

Science

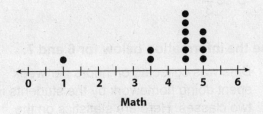

Math

9. What is the math outlier? _____

10. Find the medians.

Science: _____ Math: _____

11. Compare the ranges.

_____

Use the box plots for 12–14. They show scores for 14 students on two different chapter tests.

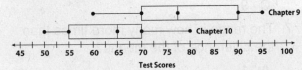

Test Scores

12. For Chapter 9, how many students got a score greater than the median score?

_____

13. What were the highest scores?

Chapter 9: _____ Chapter 10: _____

14. Which test was more difficult? Explain how you know.

_____

_____

15. A painter adds 6.5 gallons of blue paint to 5 gallons of red paint. How many total gallons of paint does he have?

_____

Statistics on temperatures for two cities are shown below. Use the data for 16 and 17.

City 1:
mean = 65
range = 15

City 2:
mean = 68
range = 15

16. What is the difference in the means?

_____

17. What is the difference in the means as a multiple of the range?

_____

18. What is $2\frac{1}{4}$ written as a decimal?

_____

MODULE 12

Experimental Probability
Module Quiz: B

1. Denise rolls a number cube that has sides labeled 1 to 6 and then flips a coin. What is the probability that she rolls an odd number and flips heads?

   A $\frac{1}{8}$ C $\frac{1}{2}$

   B $\frac{1}{4}$ D $\frac{3}{4}$

2. There are 4 jacks in a standard deck of 52 playing cards. If Patricia selects a card at random, what is the probability that it will be a jack?

   A $\frac{1}{52}$ C $\frac{1}{2}$

   B $\frac{1}{13}$ D $\frac{12}{13}$

3. The experimental probability that Kevin will catch a fly ball is equal to $\frac{7}{8}$. About what percent of the time will Kevin catch a fly ball?

   A 55%   C 77%

   B 66%   D 88%

4. Janelle's Office Supply shop sells 2 types of notebooks. Each notebook is offered in red, blue, or yellow. If a notebook is selected at random, how many different possibilities are in the sample space?

   A 4   C 8

   B 6   D 16

5. Morgan saw 10 blue, 8 red, and 42 white cars drive by her house in 1 hour. What is the experimental probability that the next car that drives by her house will **not** be a white car?

   A 0.3   C 0.6

   B 0.5   D 0.7

6. If the probability of an event is 0.99, which of the following best describes the event?

   A The event will never occur.

   B There is a small chance that the event will occur.

   C The event is likely to occur.

   D The event will definitely occur.

7. A rectangle has a width of 10 inches and a length of 12 inches. A similar rectangle has a width of 15 inches. What is the length of the similar rectangle?

   A 12 in.   C 16 in.

   B 14 in.   D 18 in.

8. The experimental probability that Jessica will hit the ball when she is at bat is $\frac{2}{5}$. If she is at ball 50 times in a season, how many times can Jessica expect to hit the ball?

   A 15   C 25

   B 20   D 30

9. Philip has a box of crayons. 45 are yellow, 12 are green, 25 are blue, and 7 are red. If Philip selects a crayon at random, which color crayon would he be **most** likely to select?

   A green   C red

   B blue   D yellow

10. Celine flipped a coin 100 times. She flipped heads 41 times and tails 59 times. What is the experimental probability that the next flip will be heads?

    A $\frac{41}{100}$ C $\frac{59}{100}$

    B $\frac{1}{2}$ D $\frac{3}{4}$

MODULE 12 **Experimental Probability**

11. A number cube has sides labeled 1 to 6. Connie rolls the number cube 12 times. She rolls a 5 three times. What is the experimental probability that her next roll will **not** be a 5?

_____

12. Suki has 54 rock songs, 92 dance songs and 12 classical songs on her playlist. If Suki's music player randomly selects a song from the playlist, what is the probability that the song will **not** be a classical song?

_____

13. **Dominick's Survey Results**

Food	Number of Students
Pizza	8
Hamburger	12
Pasta	14
Steak	6

Dominick recorded the favorite food of students in his class. Based on the results of his survey, what is the experimental probability the next student he surveys will respond "Pizza" or "Steak"?

_____

14. The experimental probability of rain in a certain town is 20 percent. In the next 45 days, how many days can one expect it to rain?

_____

15. Alessandro painted $\frac{1}{3}$ of a wall in 45 minutes. If he keeps painting at the same rate, how much longer will it take him to finish painting the wall?

_____

16. **Cathy's Color Picks**

Color	Frequency
Red	10
Yellow	5
Blue	12
Orange	28

Cathy conducted an experiment in which she placed red, yellow, blue, and orange pieces of paper in a hat and drew them out without looking. The number of times Cathy drew each color is shown in the table above. What is the experimental probability that the next slip of paper Cathy draws will be orange?

_____

17. The experimental probability that Amir will make a basket is 0.4. The experimental probability that Juju will make a basket is 0.6. If Amir and Juju each shoot 150 baskets, about how many more baskets will Juju be expected to make?

_____

18. Daria selected a number from the positive integers less than 10. What is the probability that she selected a prime number?

_____

MODULE 12

Experimental Probability

Module Quiz: D

1. L'Shanda can choose between 3 sweaters and 4 skirts. If she selects 1 sweater and 1 skirt, how many possible outcomes are in the sample space?

   A 7

   B 12

   C 81

2. At a city hospital, 40 boys and 50 girls were born yesterday. What is the experimental probability that the next baby born will be a girl?

   A $\frac{4}{9}$

   B $\frac{5}{9}$

   C $\frac{4}{5}$

3. A basket contains 20 green apples and 30 red apples. If a piece of fruit is selected at random from the basket, what is the probability that it will **not** be a red apple?

   A $\frac{2}{5}$

   B $\frac{3}{5}$

   C $\frac{2}{3}$

4. Jalil plays hockey. When Jalil takes a shot on goal, the probability that he scores is $\frac{3}{4}$. If Jalil takes 80 shots on goal in a season, how many times can he expect to score?

   A 30

   B 40

   C 60

5. A garden has 20 roses, 30 tulips, and 40 daffodils. If Selma randomly selects a flower from the garden, which flower is she **least** likely to pick?

   A Rose

   B Tulip

   C Daffodil

6. Colleen recorded the type of trees in the woods near her house. She counted 20 spruce trees and 50 maple trees. What is the experimental probability that the next tree Colleen finds will be a spruce tree?

   A $\frac{2}{7}$

   B $\frac{2}{5}$

   C $\frac{5}{7}$

7. The experimental probability that an SUV will pass by Andi's store is 0.4. If 500 cars pass by Andi's store, how many can she expect to be SUVs?

   A 20

   B 100

   C 200

8. Allison flipped a coin twenty times. She flipped heads 4 times and tails 16 times. What is the experimental probability that Allison will flip heads on her next flip?

   A $\frac{1}{5}$

   B $\frac{1}{4}$

   C $\frac{4}{5}$

MODULE 12

Experimental Probability

9. Billy is on a weekend fishing trip with his scout troop. So far he has caught 4 trout and 10 catfish. What is the probability that the next fish that Billy catches will be a catfish?

_____

10. Maggie answered 20 out of 25 questions correctly on a math test. What percent of the questions did she answer correctly?

_____

11. **Theo's Survey Results**

Gender		Eye Color	
		Brown	**Blue**
	Boy	25	25
	Girl	25	25

Theo recorded the gender and eye color of students walking in the hallway at his middle school. What is the experimental probability that the next student he sees will be a boy with brown eyes?

_____

12. A bag contains 5 red marbles and 10 blue marbles. If Jen selects a marble from the bag without looking, what is the probability that she will **not** pull out a red marble?

_____

13. At a sandwich shop, Diana can select from 2 types of bread and 5 types of meat. If she randomly selects 1 type of bread and 1 type of meat, how many possible choices does she have?

_____

14. Alicia randomly selects one number from the list of numbers below.

20, 25, 30, –35, 40

What is the probability that she selects a **positive** number?

_____

15. **Liz's Experimental Outcomes**

Trial	Outcome
1	3, Tails
2	3, Tails
3	4, Tails
4	2, Heads
5	1, Heads

Liz conducted an experiment. In each trial, she rolled a number cube that has sides labeled 1 to 6 and then flipped a coin. The results are shown above. What is the experimental probability that Liz's next flip will be tails?

_____

16. Amelie randomly picked 15 flowers from a garden. Five of the flowers she picked were tulips. What is the experimental probability that the next flower she picks will be a tulip?

_____

17. Michael recorded the color of each car that passed by his office. He saw 30 blue cars and 40 green cars. What is the experimental probability that the next car Michael sees will be a blue car?

_____

MODULE 13

Theoretical Probability and Simulations
Module Quiz: B

1. What is the probability of flipping a coin 3 times and getting 3 heads?

   A $\frac{1}{8}$ C $\frac{1}{2}$

   B $\frac{1}{4}$ D $\frac{3}{4}$

2. Two number cubes each have sides that are labeled 1 to 6. Isis rolls the 2 number cubes. What is the probability that the sum of the numbers rolled will equal 4?

   A $\frac{1}{36}$ C $\frac{1}{12}$

   B $\frac{1}{18}$ D $\frac{1}{6}$

3. Dustin has a spinner that is divided into 5 equal-size sections colored red, blue, orange, white, and green. What is the probability that Dustin spins pink on the next spin?

   A 0   C 0.5

   B 0.25   D 0.75

4. Isidro flips a fair coin 40 times. How many times can he expect heads to appear?

   A 4   C 15

   B 10   D 20

5. A number cube has sides labeled 1 to 6. Hannah rolls the number cube 18 times. How many times can she expect to roll a number less than 3?

   A 2   C 6

   B 3   D 8

6. Flavia has a bag with 8 white balls, 9 red balls, 14 green balls, and 10 orange balls. If she chooses a ball from the bag without looking, which color ball will Flavia be **least** likely to choose?

   A white   C green

   B red   D orange

7. Without looking, Tammy takes a marble out of a bag that contains 10 red marbles, 15 green marbles, and 25 blue marbles. She records its color and returns the marble to the bag. If Tammy repeats this process 90 times, how many times can she expect to pull out a red marble?

   A 5   C 15

   B 10   D 18

8. Caelin drives at 30 miles per hour. How many hours will it take him to drive 210 miles?

   A 5 h   C 7 h

   B 6 h   D 8 h

9. Alexander spins a spinner with four equally-sized regions and flips a coin. How many outcomes are possible?

   A 2   C 8

   B 6   D 36

10. Scarlett selects a card at random from a deck that contains 18 red, 12 yellow, and 20 blue cards. What is the probability that she does **not** select a red card?

    A $\frac{13}{25}$ C $\frac{18}{25}$

    B $\frac{16}{25}$ D $\frac{24}{25}$

11. Bella rolls 2 number cubes 60 times. How many times can she expect the sum of the numbers to be greater than 10?

    A 3   C 10

    B 5   D 12

12. Glen has 3 pairs of shoes, 5 shirts, and 4 pairs of pants. How many outfits consisting of 1 pair of shoes, 1 shirt, and 1 pair of pants can he make?

    A 12   C 30

    B 20   D 60

Theoretical Probability and Simulations

13. Two number cubes each have sides labeled 1 to 6. Ann rolls both number cubes. On the first roll, the sum of the numbers was equal to 10. On the second roll, the sum of the numbers was equal to 7. Which sum was more likely to occur? Explain.

_____

_____

_____

14.   **Simran's Simulation Results**

Trial	Numbers Generated	Trial	Numbers Generated
1	1, 1, 3, 3	6	4, 5, 5, 5
2	3, 4, 5, 5	7	3, 4, 4, 5
3	2, 3, 4, 4	8	2, 2, 2, 1
4	1, 3, 4, 4	9	4, 5, 5, 3
5	3, 4, 4, 5	10	3, 3, 3, 3

Simran used a simulation to predict the number of defective parts that are produced in a factory. Random numbers are generated. A number 1 indicates that the part is defective. Numbers 2, 3, 4, or 5 indicate that the part is not defective. Of the next four parts produced, what is the experimental probability that none of the parts are defective?

_____

15. Fatima bought a video game that has a regular price of $45. The game was on sale for 15 percent off, and she paid sales tax of 7 percent. What was the price Fatima paid for the video game?

_____

16. Constantine walked 4 miles in 50 minutes. If he continues walking at this pace, how many minutes will it take him to walk 6 miles?

_____

17.   **Simran's Simulation Results**

Trial	Numbers Generated	Trial	Numbers Generated
1	1, 1, 3, 3	6	4, 5, 5, 5
2	3, 4, 5, 5	7	3, 4, 4, 5
3	2, 3, 4, 4	8	2, 2, 2, 1
4	1, 3, 4, 4	9	4, 5, 5, 3
5	3, 4, 4, 5	10	3, 3, 3, 3

Simran used a simulation to predict the number of days of rain in his town. A number 1 or 2 indicates a week in which it rained. Numbers 3, 4, or 5 indicate a week in which it did not rain. The results of the simulation are shown above. What is the experimental probability that it will rain in Simran's town in at least 1 of the next 4 weeks?

_____

18. Each student in a class of 25 students wrote down a random digit. What is the predicted number of students who wrote a digit that is greater than 7?

_____

19. A special deck of cards consists of 5 red cards, 20 blue cards, and 25 green cards. Svetlana selects 1 card from the special deck 500 times. How many times can she expect to draw a red card?

_____

MODULE 13 Theoretical Probability and Simulations
Module Quiz: D

1. A number cube has sides labeled 1 to 6. Gia rolls the number cube. What is the probability that she rolls a 4?

   A $\frac{1}{8}$

   B $\frac{1}{6}$

   C $\frac{1}{3}$

2. There are 7 red cards and 13 blue cards in a deck of cards. If Yuki randomly selects a card from the deck, what is the probability that it is a red card?

   A $\frac{7}{20}$

   B $\frac{7}{13}$

   C $\frac{13}{20}$

3. Anne has 3 pairs of blue socks and 5 pairs of pink socks. If she randomly selects a pair of socks, what is the probability that it is blue?

   A $\frac{3}{8}$

   B $\frac{3}{5}$

   C $\frac{5}{8}$

4. The probability that Cori makes a basket is $\frac{3}{10}$. If she shoots 50 baskets, how many can she expect to make?

   A 15

   B 30

   C 50

5. Beatrice drives 50 miles per hour. How many hours does it take her to drive 100 miles?

   A 1 h

   B 2 h

   C 3 h

6. A spinner is divided into 4 equal sections colored red, green, blue, and orange. Ennis spins the spinner. What is the probability that he spins orange?

   A 0

   B $\frac{1}{4}$

   C $\frac{1}{2}$

7. Patrick flips a coin 100 times. How many times can he expect to flip heads?

   A 50

   B 70

   C 100

8. Syeda has a bag with 10 pink thimbles and 20 silver thimbles. If she draws a thimble from the bag without looking, what is the probability that it will be a pink thimble?

   A $\frac{1}{3}$

   B $\frac{2}{3}$

   C 1

9. Tamara bought a sweater that was on sale for 30 percent off the original price. The original price of the sweater was $80. How much did Tamara pay?

   A $24

   B $40

   C $56

MODULE 13

Theoretical Probability and Simulations

10. A standard number cube has 6 sides labeled 1 to 6. Apu rolls a standard number cube 30 times. How many times can he expect to roll a 5 or 6?

_____

11. The probability that Fadi wins a certain game of chance is $\frac{1}{3}$. Fadi plays the game 150 times. How many times can he expect to win the game?

_____

12. The train arrives on time with a probability of 0.9. If Esme takes the train 10 times, how many times can she expect it to be on time?

_____

13. Korie randomly selects a number from the numbers shown below.

    54, 60, 11, 0, 5, 7, 20

    What is the probability that the number she selects is an even number?

_____

14. Madhu can select from 3 types of oranges and 4 types of apples. If she randomly selects 1 orange and 1 apple, how many possible choices does she have?

_____

15. Dalia bought a jacket for 20 percent off the original price. The original price of the jacket was $120. How much did Dalia pay?

_____

16.

Jay's Simulation Outcomes

Trial	Numbers Generated	Trial	Numbers Generated
1	1, 1, 1, 3	6	4, 1, 5, 1
2	3, 1, 5, 5	7	1, 1, 1, 1
3	2, 3, 4, 4	8	2, 2, 2, 1
4	1, 3, 1, 4	9	4, 1, 5, 3
5	3, 4, 4, 1	10	3, 3, 1, 2

Jay used a simulation to predict the number of years in which he will see a groundhog on Groundhog Day. A number 1 indicates a year in which he will see a groundhog. Numbers 2, 3, 4, or 5 indicate a year in which he will not see a groundhog. The results of the simulation are shown above. What is the experimental probability that Jay will see a groundhog on Groundhog Day in all four of the next four years?

_____

17. A special deck of cards has 10 red cards, 20 blue cards, and 40 green cards. If Tay randomly draws a card, what is the probability that it will be green?

_____

18. A spinner is divided into 3 equal sections shaded blue, green and orange. Brody spins the spinner. If he spins the spinner 300 times, how many times can he expect the spinner to land on blue?

_____

The Number System

Unit Test: A

1. The temperature at noon was –3°C. By 10 P.M. on the same day the temperature decreased by 5.4°. What was the temperature at 10 P.M.?

   A –8.4°C   C –2.4°C

   B –5.4°C   D 1.6°C

2. Derek spends $3 on breakfast and $5.50 on lunch every school day. How much does he spend on breakfast and lunch in a school week?

   A $38.50   C $49.90

   B $42.50   D $59.50

3. What is the value of (–4.5)(–8.25)?

   A –37.125   C 3.75

   B –12.75   D 37.125

4. An artist is cutting pieces of ribbon to use in a project. Each piece he cuts measures $\frac{7}{8}$ inch. The artist cuts off 5 pieces. How many total inches of ribbon has he cut off?

   A $4\frac{1}{8}$ C $5\frac{5}{7}$

   B $4\frac{3}{8}$ D $5\frac{7}{8}$

5. An airplane took off and reached an altitude of 10,000 feet in 25 minutes. How many feet per minute, on average, did the airplane climb?

   A 400

   B 500

   C 600

   D 2,500

6. The number of students enrolled at Hill School decreased by 120 students over an 8-year period. What was the average decrease in student enrollment per year?

   A 8   C 15

   B 12   D 20

7. Alexis sold boxes of homemade granola bars for $8.50 each. It costs her $2.25 to bake and package each box of granola bars. What was her profit from selling each box of granola bars?

   A –$6.25

   B $5.38

   C $6.25

   D $10.75

8. Alexandra's backpack weighs $7\frac{5}{8}$ pounds. What is the weight of her backpack expressed as a decimal?

   A 7.13   C 7.625

   B 7.58   D 7.85

9. A sandwich costs $4.25 and a fruit drink costs $1.85. How much change will you get from a $10 bill?

   A $2.90   C $3.90

   B $3.70   D $6.10

10. Which of the following fractions is equivalent to a repeating decimal?

    A $\frac{1}{5}$ C $\frac{2}{3}$

    B $\frac{5}{8}$ D $\frac{3}{4}$

UNIT 1

The Number System

11. The elevation of New Orleans, Louisiana is on average 8 feet below sea level. The elevation of El Centro, California is 39 feet below sea level. What is the difference in elevation between the two cities?

_____

12. Jalil mixed $\frac{3}{8}$ cup of sugar with $1\frac{5}{6}$ cups of water. How many more cups of water than sugar did he use in his mixture?

_____

13. What is the product of –3.4 and 2.5?

_____

14. Fatima wants to purchase a scarf for $45.00 and a sweater for $77.50. If she currently has $100, how much more money does she need to purchase the two items?

_____

15. Arnaud paid $350 for a rug. The price of the rug that Bill purchased was $\frac{2}{5}$ the price that Arnaud paid. How much did Bill pay for his rug?

_____

16. The Martin family spent $518 on groceries in one week. What is the average amount the family spent on groceries per day?

_____

17. What is the average of –2.5, 5.2, 1.7, and –0.8?

_____

18. What is the quotient of –5.2 ÷ 3.9?

_____

19. Gail read $\frac{2}{15}$ of a book on Monday and $\frac{3}{5}$ of the book on Tuesday. What fraction of the book did she read on Monday and Tuesday?

_____

20. At Benito's school, $\frac{5}{8}$ of the students like math class. If there are 208 students, how many of them like math?

_____

21. Kevin is $5\frac{1}{2}$ feet tall. Jane is $5\frac{3}{8}$ feet tall. Who is taller? Justify your answer.

_____

22. Beatrice built about $\frac{1}{3}$ of a sandcastle. Linda built $\frac{4}{7}$ of the same castle. What fraction of the sandcastle did they build together?

_____

23. In Priya's math class there are 10 boys and 15 girls. What is the ratio of boys to girls in Priya's math class? Express your answer as a decimal.

_____

UNIT 1 — The Number System
Unit Test: B

1. What is the value of $-12 - (-35)$?

   A -47 C 23

   B -23 D 47

2. Elijah spent $5.25 for lunch every day for 5 school days. He spent $6.75 on Saturday. How much did he spend in all?

   A $26.16

   B $31.25

   C $33.00

   D $60.00

3. Briana played a trivia game in which she lost 5 points for each incorrect answer and gained 10 points for each correct answer. If Briana answered 11 questions correctly and 4 questions incorrectly, what was her total score?

   A 15   C 80

   B 70   D 90

4. What is the product of $-1\frac{3}{8}$ and $2\frac{4}{5}$ expressed as a mixed number?

   A $-3\frac{17}{20}$ C $-1\frac{17}{40}$

   B $-\frac{55}{112}$ D $3\frac{17}{20}$

5. Each year a store decreased the price of a certain model of TV by $35. If the price in 2001 was $1,950, what was the price in 2009?

   A $1,670   C $1,880

   B $1,745   D $1,915

6. What is the value of $-3\frac{2}{3} \div \frac{1}{3}$?

   A -11 C $-1\frac{2}{9}$

   B -5 D 11

7. At Daria's school, $\frac{3}{8}$ of the students are left-handed. If there are 320 students, how many of them are left-handed?

   A 37

   B 60

   C 120

   D 160

8. Benjamin had $450 in his bank account on Monday. On Tuesday he wrote five checks for $24.50 each. On Wednesday he made three deposits of $45 each. How much money was in his account after the checks and deposits cleared?

   A $192.50   C $462.50

   B $437.50   D $707.50

9. Jake's family is moving to a new home. They packed 22 boxes in $1\frac{5}{6}$ hours. What is the average number of boxes they packed per hour?

   A 10   C 12

   B 11   D 15

10. On a certain day the temperature in Seattle was $-1°C$ and the temperature in Houston was $18°C$. How many degrees lower was the temperature in Seattle?

    A 8°   C 17°

    B 9°   D 19°

11. What is the value of $-3 + 4.5 - (-1.2)$?

    A -9.2 C 0.3

    B -2.7 D 2.7

12. Alyssa rode her bicycle 14.2 miles in 0.8 hours. What is the average number of miles she rode per hour?

    A 11.36   C 17.75

    B 15.0   D 22.2

UNIT 1

The Number System

13. A jug of orange juice contains 40.75 fluid ounces. It is shared equally among 5 people. How many ounces of orange juice does each person receive?

_____

14. What is the value of $-\dfrac{7}{8} \div -1\dfrac{2}{5}$?

_____

15. There are 4,200 adults in Lakeview. Three-eighths of the adults in Lakeview do **not** have children. How many adults in Lakeview have children?

_____

16. Calvin earned $1,425 dollars by working five days in a week. He also received a bonus of $200. What is the average amount that he earned per day?

_____

17. Seth purchased a printer for $350. The price of the printer that Jose purchased was $\dfrac{4}{5}$ the price that Seth paid. How much did Jose pay for his printer?

_____

18. Timothy made 60 quarts of cider. He poured the cider into containers. Each container holds $\dfrac{4}{11}$ of a quart. How many containers did Timothy use?

_____

19. Dori bought a sandwich for $6.75, a bag of dried fruit for $1.45 and a bottle of water for $1.75. She paid the cashier with a $20 bill. How much change did she receive?

_____

20. What is the result when −2.5 is divided by 1.8?

_____

21. Alex wants to purchase a set of 9 figurines that cost $38 each. So far he has saved $240 towards this purchase. How much more money does he need to save?

_____

22. Kenneth shared a basket of apples with three of his friends. The basket weighed 14.75 pounds. What is the weight of the apples that each of the friends received?

_____

23. A test has 40 questions. Denise finished $\dfrac{2}{5}$ of the questions in the first 10 minutes and $\dfrac{1}{2}$ of the remaining questions in the next 15 minutes. How many questions had Denise answered after 25 minutes?

_____

24. George ate $\dfrac{2}{3}$ of a container of Chinese food. Silvia ate $\dfrac{1}{5}$ of the same container of Chinese food. What fraction of the container of Chinese food did they eat together?

_____

UNIT 1 The Number System

Unit Test: C

1. A sandwich costs $5.70 and a piece of fruit costs $2.15. If you have a $20 bill, how much change will you get?

   A $2.15

   B $7.85

   C $11.15

   D $12.15

2. Cole went hiking near his house. The first trail took him 7 miles away from his house. The second trail took him $3\frac{1}{2}$ miles closer to his house. The third trail took him $2\frac{2}{5}$ miles further away from his house. How many miles from his house was Cole after he finished hiking the third trail?

   A $1\frac{1}{10}$ C $8\frac{1}{10}$

   B $5\frac{9}{10}$ D $12\frac{9}{10}$

3. Dara went on vacation to New York City in 2012. She bought a $20 pass to ride the subway. Each time she rode the subway it cost her $2.25. If she rode the subway 7 times, how much money was left on her pass at the end of her trip?

   A $2.25   C $8.50

   B $4.25   D $15.75

4. Linda earns $90,000 per year. If she does not work for 2 months in a year, how much money would she earn?

   A $7,500   C $60,000

   B $15,000   D $75,000

5.

Income and Expenses for Callie's Cafe		
Month	Income	Expenses
January	$5,450	$2,220
February	$5,780	$2,750
March	$6,140	$3,030
April	$4,870	$2,140

Income and expenses for Callie's Café are shown in the table. In which month was profit the greatest?

   A January   C March

   B February   D April

6. Ms. Henning wants to purchase 30 calculators for her math class. Calculators cost $14 each. Ms. Henning currently has $300 in her account to spend on the calculators. How much more money does she need?

   A $100   C $240

   B $120   D $420

7. Working together, 5 friends collected $40\frac{5}{8}$ bags of food for the homeless. On average, how many bags of food did each friend collect?

   A $8\frac{1}{8}$ C $10\frac{1}{8}$

   B 10   D 12

8. Diamond has $350 in her bank account. She wrote 4 checks for $18.45 each and 2 checks for $51.25 each. What will be the balance in Diamond's account after the checks are cashed?

   A $102.50   C $176.30

   B $173.70   D $378.70

9. Andre rode his bicycle to a park located $5\frac{1}{2}$ miles from his house. He returned along the same route. After riding $7\frac{1}{3}$ miles total, how many more miles does Andre need to ride to reach his home?

_____

10. Anne has a $10\frac{3}{4}$ -pound bag of flour. Each time she bakes a batch of rolls she uses $2\frac{1}{6}$ pounds of flour. How many pounds of flour remain after Anne bakes 3 batches of rolls?

_____

11. Tommy wrote down all of the whole numbers greater than −1 and less than 3. What is the average value of these numbers?

_____

12. Evelyn wants to buy 5 pens that cost $2.45 each and 3 notebooks that cost $4.39 each. If she currently has $20, how much more money does she need?

_____

13. At the supermarket Cammy can buy $\frac{2}{5}$ pound of oranges for $4. At the farmer's market she can buy $\frac{4}{7}$ pound of oranges for the same price. Where does she get the better deal? Explain your answer.

_____

14. Boris buys the newspaper every morning. Weekday newspapers cost $1.50 each. Saturday papers cost $0.75 and Sunday papers cost $3.25. How much does Boris spend on newspapers each week?

_____

15. How much greater is the value of $\left(-2\frac{3}{5}\right)\left(-4\frac{1}{8}\right)$ than the value of $3\frac{3}{4} \div 1\frac{1}{5}$? Express your answer as a mixed number.

_____

16. Ji and Layla played a game in which they scored 10 points for a correct answer and lost 20 points for an incorrect answer. Ji answered 7 questions correctly and 3 questions incorrectly. Layla answered 5 questions correctly and 1 question incorrectly. Who had the higher score? By how many points?

_____

17. Jenya answered 24 out of 30 questions correctly on her math test and 21 out of 25 questions correctly on her science test. On which test did she score higher? Explain your answer.

_____

18. Tom receives an allowance of $20 per week. If he bought 3 comic books for $2.75 each and an action figure for $10.99, how much of his allowance did he have left?

_____

UNIT	**The Number System**
1	*Unit Test: D*

1. Lin read $\frac{3}{8}$ of a magazine article on Monday and $\frac{1}{8}$ of the article on Tuesday. What fraction of the article did she read on Monday and Tuesday?

   A $\frac{1}{8}$

   B $\frac{1}{4}$

   C $\frac{1}{2}$

2. Which of the following is equal to $6 - (-5)$?

   A -11

   B 1

   C 11

3. Which of the following fractions is equal to a repeating decimal?

   A $\frac{1}{3}$

   B $\frac{2}{5}$

   C $\frac{5}{8}$

4. Which of the following fractions is **not** equivalent to a repeating decimal?

   A $1\frac{2}{3}$

   B $5\frac{1}{12}$

   C $3\frac{3}{8}$

5. What is the value of $(-0.6)(-2.5)$?

   A -3.1

   B 1.5

   C 1.9

6. A baseball glove was on sale for $\frac{5}{6}$ of the original price. If the original price was $90, what was the sale price?

   A $15

   B $75

   C $108

7. What is the value of $-1.8 \div 0.2$?

   A -9

   B -1.6

   C -0.36

8. Annalee hammered a nail into a piece of wood. Each time she hammered the nail, it went $\frac{1}{8}$ inch deeper into the wood. If she hammered the nail 4 times, how deep did Annalee hammer the nail?

   A $\frac{1}{8}$ inch

   B $\frac{1}{2}$ inch

   C $\frac{5}{8}$ inch

9. Bhavesh walked $3\frac{1}{8}$ miles on Saturday and Alana walked $4\frac{3}{4}$ miles. How many more miles did Alana walk?

   A $\frac{5}{8}$ mi

   B $1\frac{1}{2}$ mi

   C $1\frac{5}{8}$ mi

10. Kyle swam 450 yards in 5 minutes. What is the average number of yards he swam per minute?

    A 45

    B 90

    C 95

UNIT 1

The Number System

11. Tony played a game in which he won 550 points after 10 rounds. What is the average number of points he won per round?

_____

12. Deedee wants to buy four pairs of shoes that cost $60.25 each. How much money does she need to save to purchase the shoes?

_____

13. What is the number $7\frac{1}{3}$ written as an improper fraction?

_____

14. Profits at Lin's Pastry shop increased by $1,750 in one 7-day week. By how much did profits increase each day?

_____

15. Kimmy went to school for $6\frac{3}{4}$ hours on Tuesday. What is $6\frac{3}{4}$ expressed as a decimal?

_____

16. During a sale, all T-shirts are $5 off. Timani used a coupon to get an additional $10 off his purchase. If the original price of a T-shirt was $30, how much did Timani pay?

_____

17. What is the value of $1 + -7 - (-2.5)$?

_____

18. Leni's calculator weighs $\frac{7}{12}$ pound. What is the weight of her calculator expressed as a decimal?

_____

19. Tamara rode her bicycle 8 miles in 0.5 hour. What was the average rate that she rode her bicycle in miles per hour?

_____

20. Jonathan went for a jog. Every time he stops to tie his shoelaces, his jog lasts $2\frac{1}{2}$ minutes longer. If he stops to tie his shoelaces four times, how much longer does his jog take?

_____

21. Ryan's Coffee Shop earned $4,500 income last week. Expenses were $4,900. What was Ryan's profit or loss for the week?

_____

22. A bagel costs $2.15 and cream cheese costs $0.75. If you buy milk for $2.00, is $5.00 enough to cover the cost of all items? Explain.

_____

23. Wally purchased a fan that was on sale for $\frac{4}{9}$ of the original price. If the original price was $180, what was the price that Wally paid?

_____

24. What is the value of $-3\frac{1}{3} \div 1\frac{1}{4}$ expressed as a mixed number?

_____

The Number System
Performance Task

Of Kites and Fishing Hooks

The heights of kites and the depths of fishing hooks can be recorded using positive and negative integers and rational numbers. Use the table below. Show your work.

Kite	Height (ft)	Fishing Hook	Depth (ft)
A	21	E	−7.1
B	35.4	F	−5.6
C	$28\frac{3}{4}$	G	$-6\frac{2}{3}$

1. Kite A is at a height of 21 feet. It ascends 15 feet. At what height is it now?

_____

2. Fishing Hook E is at −7.1 feet. It descends another 3.25 feet. What is its depth now?

_____

3. The string on Kite C is tripled. How high can Kite C fly now?

_____

4. Fishing Hook E is dropped 2.5 times its present depth. Where is Fishing Hook E now?

_____

5. What is the distance from Kite C (in Exercise 3) to Fishing Hook E (in Exercise 4)?

_____

6. Fishing Hook G is let down $2\frac{1}{2}$ times its present depth. Where is

Fishing Hook G now?

_____

7. Write your own problem using the data in the table.

_____

_____

Name _____ Date _____ Class _____

1. A machine makes 300 boxes in 15 minutes. Which expression equals the unit rate in boxes per hour?

   A 300×15 C $300 \div 15$

   B $300 \times \frac{1}{4}$ D $300 \div \frac{1}{4}$

2. The table shows a person saving money at a constant rate.

Weeks	2	4	6	8
Total Savings ($)	60	120	180	240

   How much is this person saving per week?

   A $2   C $60

   B $30   D $120

3. A student reads at a rate of 16 pages per day. Which ordered pair is **not** on the graph of this relationship?

   A (0, 16)   C (1.5, 24)

   B (1, 16)   D (2, 32)

4. Jesse bought 5.2 pounds of grapes for $7.75. Using the unit rate, how much would 3 pounds of grapes cost?

   A $1.49   C $4.47

   B $2.98   D $12.22

5. What is the percent of increase for a population that changed from 25,000 to 30,000?

   A 16.6%   C 83.3%

   B 20%   D 120%

6. A merchant buys a television for $125 and sells it for $75 more. What is the percent of markup?

   A 37.5%   C 62.5%

   B 60%   D 160%

7. How much interest is earned in 2 years on an investment of $2,000? The interest rate is 3%.

   A $60   C $600

   B $120   D $1,200

8. A quarter is what percent of a dollar?

   A 4%   C 75%

   B 25%   D 400%

9. When you find more than 100% of a number, how does your answer relate to the original number?

   A The numbers are equal.

   B It is less than the original number.

   C It is greater than the original number.

   D There is no relationship.

10. The relation of 50 squares to 100 squares can be expressed in many ways. Which of the following is **not** a way to express the relationship?

   A $\frac{5}{10}$ C 0.05

   B 50%   D 0.5

UNIT 2 **Ratios and Proportional Relationships**

11. What is the unit price if 4 pounds of fruit cost $6.48?

_____

12. The table shows the distance traveled by an object moving at a constant speed. How far will the object go in 1 minute?

Seconds	10	15	20
Meters	85	127.5	170

_____

13. Write an equation for the relationship shown on this graph.

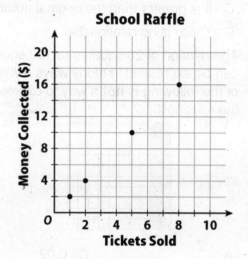

School Raffle

_____

14. Find the percent of increase from 2005 to 2010.

Year	2000	2005	2010
Population (millions)	4.3	3.2	5.6

_____

15. A keyboard that costs $475 is marked down 15% for a sale. How much is the savings?

_____

16. A shopper bought shoes marked $40. The sales tax is 8%. How much did the shopper pay in all?

_____

17. Explain why a straight line on a graph shows a constant rate of change.

_____

18. What is the constant rate of change shown in the table?

Number of Shirts	Cost ($)
1	25
2	50
3	75
8	200

19. A map scale is 1 in. : 50 mi. Two cities are 450 miles apart. How far apart are the cities on the map?

_____

20. How would you show a rate of change of 60 miles per hour on a graph? Name some of the points.

_____

| UNIT |
| 2 |

Ratios and Proportional Relationships

Unit Test: B

1. A shopper bought a 12-pound bag of oranges for $18.75. What was the unit price?

   A $0.64   C $1.73

   B $1.56   D $6.40

2. The table shows a person saving money at a constant rate.

Weeks	2	4	6	8
Total Savings ($)	60	120	180	240

   How much will this person save in 70 days?

   A $30   C $140

   B $70   D $300

3. A student reads at a rate of 16 pages per day. Which ordered pair would be on a graph of this relationship?

   A (1.5, 26)   C (5.5, 88)

   B (2.25, 30)   D (7.25, 110)

4. Denise bought 5.2 pounds of rice for $5.29. Using the unit rate, how much would 2 pounds of rice cost?

   A $1.02   C $2.04

   B $1.29   D $6.31

5. What is the percent of increase for a population that changed from 438,000 to 561,000?

   A 21.9%   C 35.6%

   B 28.1%   D 45.6%

6. A merchant buys a television for $125 and sells it for a retail price of $200. What is the markup?

   A 37.5%   C 62.5%

   B 60%   D 160%

7. $12,000 is invested for 4 years at a simple interest rate of 1.5%. How much does the investment earn?

   A $180   C $1,800

   B $720   D $7,200

8. A dime is what percent of a dollar?

   A 1%   C 100%

   B 10%   D 1.10%

9. When you find less than 100% of a number, how does your answer relate to the original number?

   A The numbers are equal.

   B It is less than the original number.

   C It is greater than the original number.

   D There is no relationship.

10. The relation of 20 squares to 100 squares can be expressed in many ways. Which of the following is **not** a way to express the relationship?

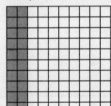

   A $\frac{2}{10}$ C 0.02

   B 20%   D 0.2

UNIT 2

Ratios and Proportional Relationships

11. A machine stamps 360 metal parts in 15 minutes. Find the unit rate in parts per hour.

_____

12. The table shows the distance traveled by an object moving at a constant speed. What is the constant of proportionality?

Seconds	10	15	20
Meters	85	127.5	170

_____

13. Write an equation for the relationship shown on this graph if the price per ticket is doubled.

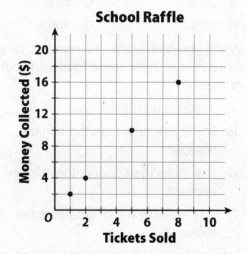

School Raffle

_____

14. Compare the percents of change.

Year	2000	2005	2010
Population (millions)	4.3	3.2	5.6

_____

15. A keyboard that costs $475 is marked down 15% for a sale. What is the reduced price of the keyboard?

_____

16. A shopper bought shoes marked $45. The sales tax is 6.5%. How much did the shopper pay in all?

_____

17. What can show a constant rate of change on a graph? Explain.

_____

18. What is the constant rate of change shown in the table?

Number of Tickets	Cost ($)
1	8
2	16
3	24
8	64

_____

19. A map scale is 1 cm : 50 km. Two cities are 3.8 cm apart. How many kilometers is it from one city to the other?

_____

20. How would you show a rate of change of 15 feet per second on a graph? Name some of the points.

_____

Name _____ Date _____ Class_____

Ratios and Proportional Relationships
Unit Test: C

1. A shopper bought a 12-pound bag of oranges for $18.75. What is the unit price per ounce?

   A $0.098   C $1.56

   B $0.64   D $9.76

2. Why does this table **not** show a proportional relationship?

Time in Weeks (x)	2	4	6	8
Savings in Dollars (y)	60	120	240	480

   A The ratio x : y equals 1 : 30.

   B The ratio x : y is not constant.

   C The savings does not stay constant.

   D The savings is not increasing fast enough.

3. When you graph a proportional relationship y = kx, what does the constant of proportionality equal?

   A x-intercept   C slope

   B y-intercept   D none of these

4. Aki bought $3\frac{3}{4}$ pounds of spinach for $6.88. Using the unit rate, how much would $1\frac{1}{2}$ pounds of spinach cost?

   A $1.83   C $3.06

   B $2.75   D $8.71

5. The population of a town doubled in 5 years, then doubled again in the next 10 years. What is the percent of increase?

   A 100%   C 300%

   B 200%   D 400%

6. The price of an item has increased 15% since last year. However, a person can buy the item for a 25% employee discount. The employee pays $172.50. What was the price last year?

   A $200   C $600

   B $270.59   D $811.79

7. $5,000 was invested at a simple interest rate. In 15 years, the account was worth 65 hundred dollars. What was the interest rate?

   A 0.2%   C 2%

   B 1.5%   D 2.15%

8. A quarter and dime make up what percent of a dollar?

   A 25%   C 70%

   B 35%   D 350%

9. When you find 215% of a number, how does your answer relate to the original number?

   A There is no relationship.

   B It is 215% less than the original number.

   C It is more than double the original number.

   D It is equal to the original number minus 215.

10. The relation of 38 squares to 100 squares can be expressed in many ways. Which of the following is **not** a way to express the relationship?

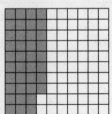

   A $\frac{19}{50}$ C 0.19

   B 38%   D 0.38

UNIT 2

Ratios and Proportional Relationships

11. A machine stamps 50 metal parts in 15 minutes 30 seconds. Find the unit rate in parts per hour.

_____

12. The table shows the distance traveled by two objects moving at constant speeds. Find their constants of proportionality. Which object is moving faster?

Time (s)	10	15	20
Object 1 (m)	85	127.5	170
Object 2 (m)	125	187.5	250

_____

13. The graph shows last year's raffle. This year the school increased prices by 50 cents per ticket. What equation represents this year's relationship?

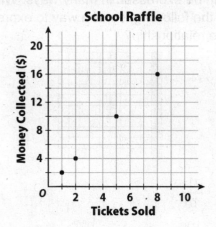

School Raffle

_____

14. In 1950, the population of a city was about 800,000 people. Over the next 50 years, the population increased to 1.3 million. Find the percent of increase.

_____

15. A business bought a lot of 2,500 lamps for fifty thousand dollars and wants to sell them at a 15% profit. How much should each lamp cost?

_____

16. A store bought a sofa wholesale for $200 and marked it up 15%. When the sofa didn't sell, they reduced the price 15%. Show why the current price is **not** $200.

_____

17. Karen is riding her bike at 4 miles per hour. She wants to show this on a graph. What should she draw?

_____

18. What is the constant rate of change shown in the table?

Number of Batteries	Cost ($)
1	1.19
2	2.38
3	3.57
8	9.52

_____

19. How would you show a rate of change of 3.5 meters per minute on a graph? Name some of the points.

_____

20. A flagpole is 20 feet tall. Its shadow is 13 feet long. A boy is standing next to the flagpole. He is 5 feet 6 inches tall. How long is his shadow?

_____

UNIT 2
Ratios and Proportional Relationships
Unit Test: D

1. A machine makes 150 boxes in 15 minutes. What is the rate?

   A 10 boxes per minute

   B 15 boxes per minute

   C 150 boxes per minute

2. A student saves $30 per month. How much is saved in 4 months?

Months	1	2	3	4
Dollars	30	60	90	

   A $4

   B $90

   C $120

3. Which ordered pair is on the line of the graph for $y = 10x$?

   A (0, 10)

   B (1, 10)

   C (10, 1)

4. Alicia bought 4 T-shirts for $23.00. Using the unit rate, how much would 6 T-shirts cost?

   A $5.75

   B $11.50

   C $34.50

5. There were 50 students in the chess club. The membership went up by 10%. How many more students joined the club?

   A 5

   B 10

   C 55

6. A cell phone costs $120 dollars. The price is reduced 30% for a sale. How much is the savings?

   A $30

   B $36

   C $70

7. A shopper buys 3 notebooks for $5 each. The percent of sales tax is 8%. How much is the sales tax?

   A $(3 \times 5) \times 0.08$

   B $(3 \times 5) \times 0.8$

   C $(3 \times 5) \times 8$

8. A quarter is what percent of a dollar?

   A 5%

   B 20%

   C 25%

9. When you find 100% of a number, how does your answer relate to the original number?

   A The numbers are equal.

   B It is less than the original number.

   C It is greater than the original number.

10. The relation of 10 squares to 100 squares can be expressed in many ways. Which of the following is **not** a way to express the relationship?

    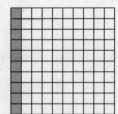

    A $\dfrac{1}{10}$

    B 10%

    C 0.01

| UNIT 2 | **Ratios and Proportional Relationships** |

11. A bag of nuts weighs 3 ounces and costs 50 cents. What is the unit price?

   50 ÷ _____ = _____ per ounce

12. A toy car travels 6 meters in 10 seconds. Complete the table to show how far the car goes in 20 seconds and 30 seconds.

Seconds	10	20	30
Meters	6		

13. Draw a line on the graph to show the proportional relationship. Then find the cost for 9 tickets.

School Raffle

_____

14. Find the percent of increase.

Year	2005	2010
Population (millions)	3.2	5.6

   (5.6 – 3.2) ÷ 3.2 = _____ = _____

15. A keyboard that costs $400 is marked down 10% for a sale. What is the reduced price of the keyboard?

   100% – 10% = _____

   90% of _____ = _____

16. A shopper bought shoes marked $40. The sales tax rate is 5%. How much is the sales tax?

   _____

17. Pete graphs the following points on a graph: (0, 0), (1, 3), and (2, 6) to show that he walks at the rate of 3 miles an hour. When he connects the points, what does he get?

   _____

18. What is the constant rate of change shown in the table?

Number of Books	Cost ($)
1	9
2	18
3	27
8	72

   _____

19. On a map, $\frac{1}{4}$ inch stands for 100 miles.

   Two cities are 3 inches apart on the map. How many miles apart are they?

   _____

20. How would you show a rate of change of 15 miles per hour on a graph? Name some of the points.

   _____

   _____

Ratios and Proportional Relationships

Performance Task

UNIT 2

In the Doghouse
Two companies, Barkly and Woof-Woof, both sell doghouses. The cost of each doghouse depends on the size of its base.

Use the table and the blank graph below for 1–4.

1. Barkly Doghouses charges $50 per square meter for their doghouses. Complete the table to show this proportional relationship.

Size (m²)	0.5	1	2.5	4
Cost ($)				

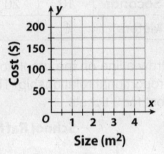

2. Graph the proportional relationship.

3. Write an equation to show the relationship in your table and graph. Use *x* for size and *y* for cost.

_____

4. Woof-Woof Doghouses charges half as much per square meter as Barkly. Draw the graph for Woof-Woof. Label both graphs with their equations.

5. Barkly Doghouses increased their prices by 10%. Complete the chart below to show their new prices.

Size (m²)	0.5	1	2.5	4
Cost ($)				

6. How will the graph change?

_____

7. Write an equation to show the new relationship.

_____

8. Woof-Woof decided to increase their prices by 40%. Complete the table to show their increased prices.

Size (m²)	0.5	1	2.5	4
Cost ($)				

9. The town has decided to add a sales tax of 2.3%. Using the new price and the town tax, calculate the cost of a 2 square-meter doghouse from each company.

_____

Expressions, Equations, and Inequalities
Unit Test: A

1. Which equation below matches the relationship shown in the table?

x	0	1	2
y	0.5	3.5	6.5

   A $y = 2x + 0.5$ C $y = 3x$
   B $y = 2x + 2$ D $y = 3x + 0.5$

2. Which value of x satisfies the equation below?

$$4x - 7 = 25$$

   A $x = -8$ C $x = 8$
   B $x = 4.5$ D $x = 32$

3. The equation $y = 15x + 500$ represents the amount y that Lin earns by working for x hours, plus a performance bonus. What is Lin's hourly rate?

   A $10   C $50
   B $15   D $500

4. What is the solution to the inequality below?

$$2x + 10 \leq 40$$

   A $x \leq 10$ C $x \geq 10$
   B $x \leq 15$ D $x \geq 15$

5. What is the solution to the equation below?

$$\frac{x}{-3} = 4$$

   A $x = -7$ C $x = -1$
   B $x = -12$ D $x = -\frac{4}{3}$

6. Which table represents the same linear relationship as $y = 2x - 5$?

A
x	0	2	4
y	−5	−1	3

B
x	0	2	4
y	−5	1	3

C
x	0	2	4
y	2	−1	3

D
x	0	2	4
y	2	2	3

7. Which of the following inequalities has the graphed solution below?

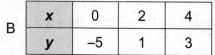

$$-4\ -3\ -2\ -1\ \ 0\ \ 1\ \ 2\ \ 3\ \ 4$$

   A $x + 1 \geq 0$ C $x + 1 \leq 0$
   B $x - 1 \geq 0$ D $x - 1 \leq 0$

8. Which equation has $x = -2$ as the solution?

   A $2x + 10 = 14$ C $3x + 10 = 1$
   B $2x + 8 = 4$ D $3x - 8 = 7$

9. Boris currently has $1,200 in his savings account. He saves $25 per month. He saves the same amount each month and does not take any money out of the account. In how many months will Boris have $1,450?

   A 10   C 15
   B 12   D 25

10. Kayla tutors a student for $18.50 per hour. She spends $50 on transportation. How much does she earn if she tutors for x hours?

   A $18.50x - 50$ C $50x - 18.50$
   B $18.50x + 50$ D $50x + 18.50$

UNIT 3

Expressions, Equations, and Inequalities

11. A technician charges an initial fee of $300 plus an hourly fee of $60. Mr. Jenks paid the technician $480. How many hours did the technician work?

_____

12. What value of x satisfies $3x + 2 = 14$?

_____

13. Draw a number line to represent the inequality $x \le -4$.

_____

14. Complete the inequality to represent the situation on the number line.

$\dfrac{x}{-4} \ge$ _____

15. Jana paid a $75 initial fee to join a sports club and a monthly fee of $15 per month. Write an expression that shows how much Jana spends after x months of membership at the sports club.

_____

Use the table for 16–18.

Cost of Purchasing Calculators

Number of Calculators	1	2	3	4
Price ($)	20	25	30	35

An electronics store charges a shipping fee plus a price per calculator. The cost of purchasing calculators is shown in the table.

16. What is the price per calculator?

_____

17. What is the shipping cost on each order?

_____

18. Write a linear relationship that shows the relationship between the cost and the number of calculators purchased.

_____

19. Jasmine paid $25 for two binders and one pack of pens. The pack of pens costs $5. What is an equation you can use to find the price of each binder?

_____

20. Kenny wrote the equation for a linear relationship shown below.

$$y = -3x + 4$$

If x equals 7, what is the value of y?

_____

21. Joey earns $16 per hour as a telemarketer. He also earns a monthly bonus of $400. Joey earned $2,000 last month. How many hours did he work?

_____

UNIT 3	**Expressions, Equations, and Inequalities**

Unit Test: B

1. Which equation matches the relationship shown in the table?

m	0	2	3
n	−0.3	3.7	5.7

   A $n = 2m - 0.3$ C $n = m - 0.3$

   B $n = 2m + 0.3$ D $n = m + 0.3$

2. Which value of x satisfies the equation below?

$$-2x - 7 = 12$$

   A $x = -9.5$ C $x = 9$

   B $x = -9$ D $x = 9.5$

3. Allison earns a $40,000 base salary plus a commission equal to 15% of her total sales. If she earned $70,000 last year, what were her total sales?

   A $6,000   C $20,000

   B $11,250   D $200,000

4. What is the solution to the inequality below?

$$4x - 3 \le -5$$

   A $x \le -0.5$ C $x \ge -0.5$

   B $x \le 0.5$ D $x \ge 0.5$

5. What is the solution to the equation below?

$$\frac{y}{-4} = 2$$

   A 2   C 8

   B −2   D −8

6. Which table represents the same linear relationship as $y = 0.25x - 10$?

A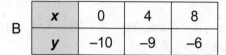

x	0	4	8
y	−10	−9	−8

B

x	0	4	8
y	−10	−9	−6

C

x	0	4	8
y	−10	−11	−12

D

x	0	4	8
y	−10	−11	−8

7. Which inequality has the graphed solution below?

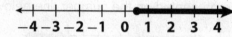

   A $2x + 1 \ge 0$ C $3x + 1 \le 0$

   B $2x - 1 \ge 0$ D $3x - 1 \le 0$

8. Alessandro currently has $2,400 in his savings account. He saves $250 per month. Bea currently has $1,750 in her account. She saves $350 per month. How much more money than Alessandro will Bea have after 12 months?

   A $100   C $550

   B $450   D $650

9. Omar mows lawns for $9.25 an hour. He spends $7.50 on gas for the mower. How much does he make if he works h hours?

   A $h + 9.25$ C $9.25h + 7.50$

   B $h + 7.50$ D $9.25h - 7.50$

Expressions, Equations, and Inequalities

10. A computer repairman charges an initial fee of $100 plus an hourly fee of $75. Mr. Billings paid the repairman $475. How many hours did the repairman work?

_____

11. If $2a - 8 = 4$ and $3b - 8 = 10$, what is the value of $a + b$?

_____

12. Draw a number line to represent the inequality $4 \geq x$.

13. Complete the inequality for the situation represented on the number line below.

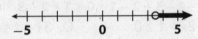

$2x >$ _____

14. Jessique sells handbags for $50 each. She spends $4 per handbag for materials and $1,000 to rent a store each month. Write an expression that shows how much profit Jessique will earn in one month if she sells x handbags.

_____

15. Jenya paid $40 per month for a cell phone plus $1.25 for each international text message she sent. She sent 50 international text messages in a month. What was Jenya's total cell phone bill?

_____

Use the table for 16–18.

Cost of Parking

Number of Hours	1	2	3	4
Price ($)	12.50	16.00	19.50	23.00

A parking garage charges an initial fee plus an hourly rate. The prices are shown in the table above.

16. What is the initial fee at the parking garage?

_____

17. What is the hourly rate for parking?

_____

18. Write a linear equation that shows the relationship between the cost and the number of hours parked.

_____

19. Cole paid $24 for two calculators and one pack of pens. Kai paid $45 for three calculators and two packs of pens. Cole and Kai both paid $6 for each pack of pens. How much more did Kai pay for each calculator?

_____

20. Jordana wrote the equation for a linear relationship as $y = -8x - 4$. For what value of x is y equal to -16?

_____

21. Carmen earns a base salary of $125,000, a commission of 4% of her total sales, and a performance bonus of $25,000. If her total compensation last year was more than $350,000, what was the least her total sales could be?

_____

UNIT 3 Expressions, Equations, and Inequalities
Unit Test: C

1. Which equation below matches the relationship shown in the table?

p	0	1	2	5
q	−1.7	−1.4	−1.1	−0.2

  A $q = p − 1.7$

  B $q = 0.3p − 1.7$

  C $q = 2p − 1.7$

  D $q = 0.4p − 1.7$

2. Jill earns a yearly salary of $40,000 plus 15% commission on total sales. Shonda earns a $55,000 yearly salary plus 10% commission on total sales. If Jill and Shonda each have sales of $750,000, how much more total income does Jill earn for the year?

  A $22,500

  B $37,500

  C $130,000

  D $152,000

3. What is the solution to the inequality below?

$$-3x − 14 \leq −5$$

  A $x \leq −3$ C $x \geq −3$

  B $x \leq 3$ D $x \geq 3$

4. What is the solution to the nearest tenth to the equation below?

$$0.3y = −2$$

  A   0.6   C   −6

  B   −6.7   D   6.7

5. Which table below represents the same linear relationship as $y = 0.15x − 8$?

A

x	0	2	4
y	−8	−7.7	−6.8

B

x	0	4	8
y	−8	−7.4	−6.8

C

x	0	5	8
y	−8	−7.2	−6.8

D

x	0	6	8
y	−8	−7.8	−6.7

6. Which inequality has the graphed solution below?

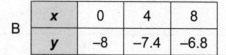

  A $−2x − 4 \geq −5$ C $2x − 4 \leq −5$

  B $−2x − 4 \geq 5$ D $2x − 4 \leq 5$

7. Antonia currently has $4,500 in her savings account. She saves $150 per month. Cal currently has $3,400 in his account. He saves $250 per month. How much more money than Antonia will Cal have after 12 months?

  A $100   C $6,300

  B $250   D $6,400

8. Which of the following values of x is **not** a solution to the inequality $−5x − 1 \leq −9$?

  A   1   C   3

  B   2   D   4

9. How many positive integers are in the solution set of the inequality below?

$$-2x + 1 \geq −6$$

  A   one

  B   two

  C   three

  D   infinitely many

Expressions, Equations, and Inequalities

10. Mike and Joe are both plumbers. Mike charges an initial fee of $100 plus an hourly fee of $60. Joe charges an initial fee of $50 plus an hourly fee of $75. If Mike and Joe each have 3-hour jobs, who earns more money? How much more?

_____

11. If $4a - 1 = 5$ and $2b - 8 = 17$, what is the value of $a + b$?

_____

12. Draw a number line to represent the inequality $\dfrac{-x}{4} \le 1$.

_____

13. Complete the inequality for the number line below.

$\dfrac{-x}{2} \ge$ _____

14. The perimeter of a rectangle is less than or equal to 50 inches. The length of the rectangle is 10 inches. What inequality represents the possible values of the width of the rectangle?

_____

Use the table for 15–17.

Number of Hours	1	2	3	4
Price ($)	22.50	29.25	36.00	42.75

A sailboat rental company charges an initial fee plus an hourly rate to rent sailboats. The costs are shown in the table above.

15. What is the initial fee to rent a sailboat?

_____

16. What is the hourly rate to rent a sailboat?

_____

17. Write a linear equation that shows the relationship between the cost and the number of hours of the sailboat rental.

_____

18. Britney paid $4.50 for two mangoes and one bag of grapes. Finn paid $9.25 for three mangoes and two bags of grapes. Britney and Finn both paid $1.25 for each mango. How much more did Finn pay for a bag of grapes?

19. Mr. Jacobs has a $200 budget for school supplies. He purchased 12 reams of printer paper for $4 each and six packs of dry-erase markers for $3 each. He will spend the rest of his budget on calculators, which cost $8 each. Write and solve an inequality that represents the number of calculators he can purchase.

_____

Name _____ Date _____ Class_____

1. Which equation matches the relationship shown in the table?

r	0	1	2
s	1.5	3.5	5.5

   A $s = r + 1.5$

   B $s = 2r + 1.5$

   C $s = 1.5r$

2. Which value of x satisfies the equation below?

$$2x + 10 = 50$$

   A 10   C 30

   B 20

3. The equation below represents the amount y that Kevin earns by working at a bakery for x hours, plus a holiday bonus.

$$y = 9x + 200$$

   What is Kevin's hourly rate?

   A $9   C $200

   B $18

4. Denise has $250 in her checking account. Each time she buys a bottle of water, she spends $2. If Denise buys x bottles of water, how much money will remain in her account?

   A $250 - 2x$

   B $2 - 250x$

   C $250 + 2x$

5. What is the solution to the inequality below?

$$x + 2 < 5$$

   A $x < 3$

   B $x > 3$

   C $x = 3$

6. If $5x + 15 = 45$, what is the value of x?

   A 5   C 15

   B 6

7. Which table represents the same linear relationship as $y = x + 3$?

A
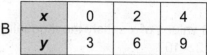
x	0	2	4
y	3	6	5

B
x	0	2	4
y	3	6	9

C
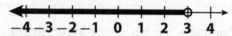
x	0	2	4
y	3	5	7

8. Which of the following inequalities has the graphed solution below?

   (number line with open circle at 3, arrow pointing left, from -4 to 4)

   A $x < 3$

   B $x > 3$

   C $x + 1 > 3$

9. Which of the following equations has $x = 4$ as the solution?

   A $2x = 8$

   B $3x = 9$

   C $4x = 20$

10. Adrian currently has $500 in his savings account. He saves $10 per month. He saves the same amount each month and does not take any money out of the account. In how many months will Adrian have $700?

   A 20

   B 50

   C 70

11. Damien earns money walking dogs. He charges $4.50 per walk. How many times does he need to walk dogs to earn $45?

   A 5

   B 9

   C 10

Expressions, Equations, and Inequalities

12. A plumber charges an initial fee of $200 plus an hourly fee of $50. Mr. Collins paid the plumber $450. How many hours did the plumber work?

_____

13. What values of x satisfy the inequality $4x + 2 > 10$?

_____

14. Draw a number line to represent the inequality $x \geq -3$.

_____

15. Complete the inequality to represent the number line.

$x + 1 \leq$ _____

16. Fatima paid a $50 initiation fee to join a gym. She also pays a fee of $25 per month. Write an expression that shows how much Fatima has spent after x months of membership at the gym.

_____

17. The table below shows the cost of purchasing computers.

Cost of Purchasing Computers

Number of Computers	1	2	3	4
Cost ($)	500	1,000	1,500	2,000

Describe a pattern in the row that shows the cost of the computers.

_____

18. Priya paid $11 for two notebooks and one pack of pencils. The pack of pencils costs $4. What equation can she write to find the price of each notebook?

_____

19. Prices of theater tickets are shown in the table below.

Cost of Theater Tickets

Number of Tickets	2	3	4
Cost ($)	$42.50	$63.75	$85

What is the price of one ticket?

_____

20. Gennifer wrote the equation for a linear relationship below.

$$y = 3x + 5$$

If x equals 9, what is the value of y?

_____

21. Alicia earns more than $12 per hour at her job at the bookstore. Write an inequality to show the least amount of money Alicia will earn for working x hours.

_____

UNIT 3

Expressions, Equations, and Inequalities
Performance Task

Jessica's Cell Phone Plan

Number of Text Messages	50	75	100	125
Cost ($)	35.00	35.75	36.50	37.25

1. Jessica's cell phone plan charges her a monthly fee plus a charge for each text message she sends. The cost of her cell phone is shown in the table above. How much does Jessica pay for each text message? Show your work.

   _____

   _____

2. What is the monthly fee for Jessica's plan if she does not send any text messages? Show your work.

   _____

   _____

3. What is an equation that shows the monthly fee, *m*, based on the number of text messages sent, *t*?

   _____

   _____

4. Jessica's bill last month was $77.00. Use the equation you wrote in Exercise 3 to find the number of text messages Jessica sent last month. Show your work.

   _____

   _____

5. Jessica wants to spend less than $80.00 per month on her cell phone. Write and solve an inequality that shows how many text messages Jessica must limit herself to in order to keep her monthly bill less than $80.00. Show your work.

   _____

   _____

6. Jessica has the option to switch to a plan that charges $65.00 per month with unlimited text messages. Jessica typically sends about 900 text messages per month. Does it make sense for her to switch to the new plan? Explain.

   _____

   _____

Geometry

UNIT 4

Unit Test: A

1. This scale drawing shows a parking lot. What is the length of the longer side of the actual lot?

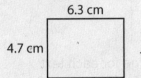

6.3 cm

4.7 cm

scale
1 cm : 50 m

  A 63 meters   C 315 meters

  B 235 meters   D 630 meters

2. Two sides of a triangle measure 10 cm and 15 cm. Which of the following is long enough to be the measure of the third side?

  A 1 cm   C 4 cm

  B 3 cm   D 6 cm

3. What is the shape of the cross section in the figure below?

  A triangle   C circle

  B square   D rectangle

4. What is the measure of $\angle GAB$?

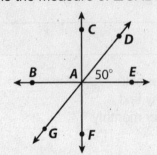

  A 40°   C 90°

  B 50°   D 130°

5. What is the circumference of the circle below?

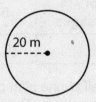

20 m

  A 62.8 m   C 345.7 m

  B 125.6 m   D 725.5 m

6. What is the area of the circle below?

18 m

  A 81 m^2 C 324 m^2

  B 254.3 m^2 D 508.7 m^2

7. What is the area of the figure below?

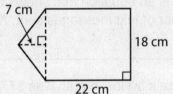

7 cm   18 cm

22 cm

  A 154 cm^2 C 459 cm^2

  B 396 cm^2 D 522 cm^2

Use the diagram for 8–9.

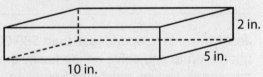

2 in.

5 in.

10 in.

8. What is the surface area of the rectangular prism shown above?

  A 100 in^2 C 200 in^2

  B 160 in^2 D 220 in^2

9. What is the volume of the rectangular prism shown above?

  A 100 in^3 C 150 in^3

  B 120 in^3 D 200 in^3

10. A map scale is 1 in. : 50 mi. Two cities are 450 miles apart. How far apart are the cities on the map?

_____

11. In the space below, draw a triangle with angles 60° and 60°, and an included side length of 1 inch.

12. Describe the cross section of the rectangular prism by naming its shape.

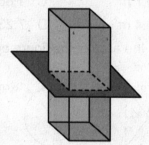

_____

13. What is the measure of ∠QPU?

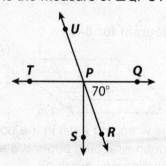

_____

14. What is the circumference of the circle below?

_____

15. What is the area of the circle below?

_____

16. What is the area of the figure below?

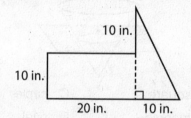

_____

Use the diagram for 17–18.

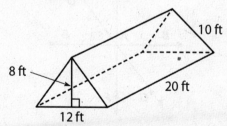

17. What is the surface area of the triangular prism shown above?

_____

18. What is the volume of the triangular prism shown above?

_____

Geometry

Unit Test: B

1. This scale drawing shows a parking lot with an actual length of 315 meters. What is the scale?

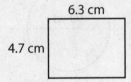

6.3 cm
4.7 cm

A   1 cm: 10 m   C   1 cm: 63 m

B   1 cm: 50 m   D   1 cm: 100 m

2. Two sides of a triangle measure 15 cm and 21 cm. Which of the following could be the measure of the third side?

A   4 cm   C   6 cm

B   5 cm   D   7 cm

3. The cone below is intersected by a horizontal plane. What is the shape of the cross section?

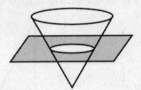

A   square   C   circle

B   triangle   D   oval

4. What is the measure of ∠GAB?

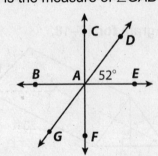

A   38°   C   89°

B   52°   D   128°

5. A circular fish pond is shown below. What is the circumference of the pond?

31 m

A   97.3 m   C   320.3 m

B   194.7 m   D   961.5 m

6. The figure below shows a circular driveway. What is the area of the driveway?

48 m

A   150.7 m^2 C   1,808.6 m^2

B   301.4 m^2 D   7,234.6 m^2

7. What is the area of the figure below? Use 3.14 for π.

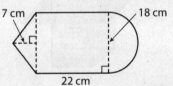

7 cm   18 cm

22 cm

A   127.2 cm^2 C   586.2 cm^2

B   396 cm^2 D   649 cm^2

Use the diagram for 8–9.

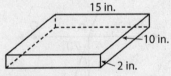

15 in.
10 in.
2 in.

8. Malia is wrapping a gift in the box above. How much wrapping paper will she need, not including any overlap?

A   300 in^2 C   400 in^2

B   340 in^2 D   550 in^2

9. What is the volume of the gift box?

A   300 in^3 C   400 in^3

B   360 in^3 D   430 in^3

10. A map scale is 1 cm : 50 km. Two cities are 3.8 cm apart. Find the actual distance between the two cities.

_____

11. In the space below, draw a triangle with angles 35° and 75°, and an included side length of 1 inch.

12. Describe the cross section of the pentagonal prism by naming its shape.

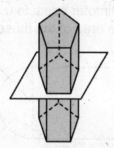

13. If m∠QPS = 90°, what is the measure of ∠RPS?

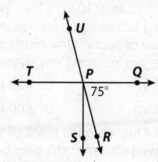

_____

14. A horse trainer walks a horse around the circular track shown below. What is the circumference of the track?

98 yd

_____

15. A landscaper mows a circle in a grass field. What is the area of the circle?

46 ft

_____

16. What is the area of the figure below?

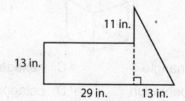

11 in.
13 in.
29 in.   13 in.

Use the diagram for 17–18.

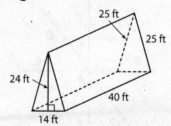

25 ft
25 ft
24 ft
40 ft
14 ft

17. A circus tent has the dimensions shown above. What is the surface area of the tent, not including the floor?

_____

18. What is the volume of the circus tent?

Geometry
Unit Test: C

1. A student enlarged this rectangle to fill as much as possible of an 8.5 cm × 11 cm piece of paper. What scale was used?

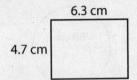

6.3 cm

4.7 cm

A 1 : 1.75   C 1 : 4.43

B 1 : 2.34   D 1 : 5.94

2. Rhonda is drawing a 3-inch square inside an isosceles triangle with two side lengths measuring 7 inches and 14 inches. Which of the following is the length of the third side of the triangle?

A 7 in.   C 12 in.

B 9 in.   D 14 in.

3. The cross section of a cube can be in all of the following shapes EXCEPT:

A triangle   C hexagon

B pentagon   D octagon

4. Suppose segment *AC* is the same length as segment *DA*, and m∠*CDA* = 71°. What is the measurement of ∠*DAE*?

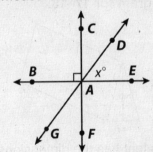

A 38°   C 71°

B 52°   D 90°

5. A baker is decorating the top of a round cake with cherries. The diameter of the cake is 9.5 inches. Each cherry is 0.75 inches in diameter. About how many cherries will the baker need to decorate the circumference of the top of the cake?

A 14   C 29

B 19   D 39

6. A contractor is tiling the bottom of a round fishpond with 1-inch square tiles that cost $0.04 each. The fishpond has a diameter of 120 inches. How much will the contractor spend on tiles?

A $30.02   C $756.09

B $452.16   D $1,304

7. The figure below shows the first floor plan of a museum. The plan is drawn to scale with 1 centimeter equal to 0.8 meters. What is the area of the museum's first floor?

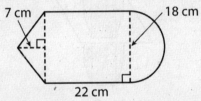

7 cm   18 cm

22 cm

A 153.4 m^2 C 375.1 m^2

B 293.7 m^2 D 468.9 m^2

8. Imani sells shirts packed in boxes that are each 15 in. × 10 in. × 2 in. Imani stacked 3 boxes and wrapped them with one piece of paper. How much paper did she use, not including any overlap?

A 300 in^2 C 420 in^2

B 340 in^2 D 600 in^2

9. Imani put the wrapped stack of three boxes inside a larger shipping box that is 17 in. × 11 in. × 7 in. What is the difference in volume between the wrapped stack of boxes and the shipping box?

A 102 in^3 C 900 in^3

B 409 in^3 D 1,309 in^3

UNIT 4 **Geometry**

10. The greatest distance across the continental United States is a bit less than 5,000 km. To fit a map on an 8.5 in. × 11 in. piece of paper, what scale should you use? Give your answer in metric units. Show why your answer works.

_____

11. A triangle has angles 39° and 47°, and an included side length of 1.75 inch. What are the measures of the third angle and the other two sides?

_____

12. A tetrahedron is shown below. It has four faces and each face is an equilateral triangle. On the figure below, draw a cross section of the tetrahedron that is in the shape of a square.

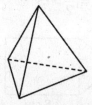

13. Three roads meet as shown in the diagram below. Local laws prohibit planting trees at corners where roads intersect at angle of less than 20°. Can a tree be planted at angle *A*? Why or why not?

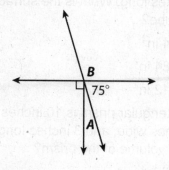

_____

14. Earth's diameter at the equator is 7,926 miles. A jet flies 550 miles per hour. How long would it take a jet to fly halfway around the equator?

_____

15. A pizza is 14 inches in diameter. Each square inch of pizza has 14.04 calories. If each slice contains about 270 calories, how many slices is the pizza cut into?

_____

16. A painter designs a mural with the shape shown below. One pint of paint will cover 50 square feet. How many whole pints of paint will the painter need to paint the mural?

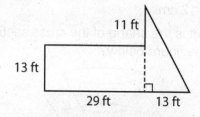

_____

17. A circus tent is in the shape of a triangular prism. The surface area of the tent is 2,896 ft², including the floor. The triangular sides of the tent measure 25 feet, 25 feet, and 14 feet. The tent is 40 feet long. What is the height of the tent?

_____

18. The tent has a fan that is suitable for cooling spaces of up to 6,560 cubic feet. Is the fan powerful enough to cool the tent? Explain why or why not.

_____

UNIT
4

Geometry
Unit Test: D

1. This is a scale drawing of a field. The scale is 1 in. : 10 ft. What is the actual length of the longer side of the field?

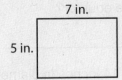

7 in.

5 in.

   A 10 ft

   B 50 ft

   C 70 ft

2. A triangle's two shortest sides measure 4 cm and 6 cm. The third side must be less than the sum of the two shorter sides. How long could the third side be?

   A 9 cm

   B 10 cm

   C 12 cm

3. What is the shape of the cross section in the figure below?

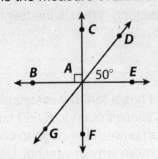

   A triangle

   B square

   C circle

4. What is the measure of $\angle DAC$?

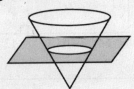

   A 40°

   B 50°

   C 90°

5. A circle has a radius of 5 meters. What is its circumference? Use the formula $C = 2\pi r$. Use 3.14 for π.

   A 5.1 m

   B 10.4 m

   C 31.4 m

6. What is the area of the circle below? Use the formula $A = \pi r^2$. Use 3.14 for π.

8 m

   A 50.2 m^2

   B 64.2 m^2

   C 128.2 m^2

7. What is the area of the figure below? (*Hint:* The formula for the area of a triangle is $A = \frac{1}{2}bh$.)

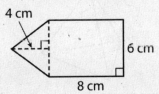

4 cm

6 cm

8 cm

   A 48 cm^2

   B 60 cm^2

   C 192 cm^2

8. A cube is 8 inches tall, 8 inches wide, and 8 inches long. What is the surface area of the cube?

   A 64 in^2

   B 384 in^2

   C 512 in^2

9. A rectangular prism is 10 inches tall, 7 inches wide, and 3 inches long. What is the volume of the prism?

   A 70 in^3

   B 120 in^3

   C 210 in^3

UNIT 4 **Geometry**

10. On a map, 1 inch stands for 100 miles. Two cities are 3 inches apart on the map. How many miles apart are they?

_____

11. Tell whether you can make a unique triangle or no triangle with sides measuring 5 cm, 4 cm, and 20 cm.

_____

12. Draw the shape of the cross section of the prism shown. Use the space next to the prism.

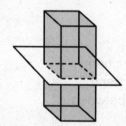

13. What is the measure of ∠SPT?

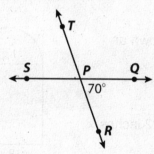

_____

14. What is the circumference of a circle with a diameter of 9 yards? Use the formula $C = 2\pi r$. Use 3.14 for π.

_____

15. What is the area of the circle below? Use the formula $A = \pi r^2$. Use 3.14 for π.

16. What is the area of the figure below?

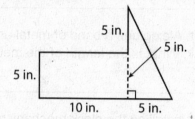

Use the diagram for 17–18.

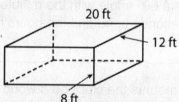

17. What is the surface area of the prism shown above? Solve the equation to find out.

$$S = Ph + 2B$$
$$= (64)(8) + 2(240)$$
$$= ?$$

_____

18. The volume of a prism is the area of its base times its height. What is the volume of the prism shown above?

_____

Geometry

Performance Task

UNIT 4

Answer the questions.

1. Alex is making a clock to give to his grandfather. To make the clock, he saws a slice of wood from a cylindrical log. What is the shape of the cross section of the log?

   _____

2. Alex then paints the face of the clock with white paint. It has a diameter of 14 inches. What is the area of the clock face?

   _____

3. Next, Alex glues a band of metal around the circumference of the clock. What is the length of the metal band?

   _____

4. After installing the clock mechanism, Alex positions the hours hand and minutes hand on the clock to show 12:30. The seconds hand forms a 60° angle with the minutes hand. What is the angle between the seconds hand and the hours hand?

   _____

5. Alex mounts the clock on a wood base with the shape shown at the right. What is the area of the wood base?

   _____

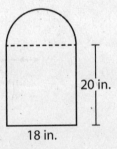

20 in.

18 in.

6. Since the clock is a gift, Alex puts it in a box. The box is 22 inches × 4 inches × 20 inches. What is the volume of the box?

   _____

7. Alex then wraps the box in wrapping paper. How much wrapping paper does Alex use, not including any overlap?

   _____

8. Finally, Alex is ready to deliver the gift. On a map, it is 2.5 inches between Alex's town and his grandfather's town. The scale on the map is 1 in. : 12 miles. What is the actual distance between the towns?

   _____

Name _____ Date _____ Class_____

UNIT 5

Statistics

Unit Test: A

Use the dot plots for 1 and 2.

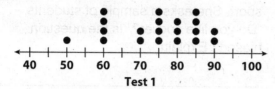
Test 1

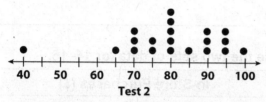
Test 2

The dot plots show 20 scores on two different tests.

1. What is the difference in the ranges?

  A 5 points   C 20 points

  B 10 points   D 35 points

2. Which test has a greater median?

  A Test 1

  B Test 2

  C They have the same median.

  D You cannot tell from the dot plots.

Use the box plots for 3 and 4.

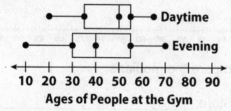
Daytime

Evening

Ages of People at the Gym

3. What are the two medians?

  A 10 and 10

  B 30 and 35

  C 40 and 50

  D 70 and 65

4. Which group has a wider spread?

  A Daytime people

  B Evening people

  C They have the same number.

  D You cannot tell from the box plots.

5. A sample is being chosen for a survey to find out how people feel about adding more stop signs near a school. Which group would be **least** biased?

  A voters

  B drivers

  C students

  D teachers

6. A random sample of 50 was taken from a shipment of 12,000 light bulbs. There were 2 broken bulbs in the sample. How many broken bulbs would you expect in the entire shipment?

  A 240   C 2,400

  B 480   D 4,800

7. A toy company uses a random sample to simulate 10 toys to inspect out of 1,000. The integers 1 to 5 represent toys that are below standard.

| 76 | 68 | 32 | 2 | 14 |
| 35 | 93 | 61 | 21 | 51 |

Based on this sample, how many toys will be below standard?

  A 1   C 10

  B 5   D 100

8. In the box plots below, the IQR is 2. Which statement about the data is true?

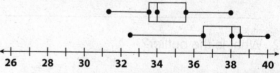

  A The difference between the medians is about 2 times the IQR.

  B The difference between the medians is about 3 times the IQR.

  C The difference between the medians is about 4 times the IQR.

  D The difference between the medians is about 5 times the IQR.

UNIT 5 **Statistics**

9. A real estate agent uses a random sample to estimate the average family size in the neighborhood. The circled numbers represent the agent's random sample.

6	1	3	4	6
5	6	5	4	8
7	3	4	7	5

(6, 5, 4, 7, 3 are circled)

Use the mean of the random sample to estimate the average family size in the entire neighborhood.

_____

Use this random sample for 10–12. It shows the number of items each person checked out at a library.

Library Items Checked Out
2, 3, 13, 3, 2, 2, 3, 6, 1, 2, 6

10. Make a dot plot.

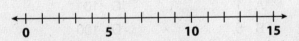

11. Find the range and median.

_____

12. What is the outlier?

_____

13. Tia wants to find out students' favorite sport. She asks a sample of students, "Do you like soccer?" Is the question biased? Explain.

_____

_____

Use the two sets of data for 14–16.

In-Store Purchases ($)
30, 34, 35, 37, 38, 46, 48, 52, 53, 56, 64, 64, 71, 80, 82

Online Purchases ($)
46, 50, 52, 52, 53, 58, 60, 61, 64, 65, 74, 75, 77, 80, 88

14. A box plot for In-Store Purchases is shown below. Use the other number line below to make another box plot to show Online Purchases.

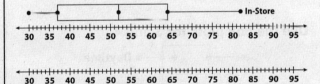

15. Compare the medians.

In-Store: _____

Online: _____

16. How would you compare these samples?

_____

_____

UNIT 5

Statistics

Unit Test: B

Use the dot plots for 1 and 2.

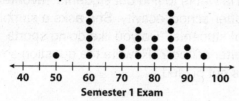

Semester 1 Exam

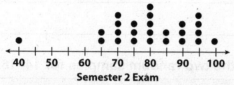

Semester 2 Exam

The dot plots show exam scores for 25 students.

1. Which exam has an outlier?

   A Semester 1   C both exams

   B Semester 2   D neither

2. What are the medians for the Semester 1 exam and the Semester 2 exam?

   A 75 and 79.8

   B 75 and 80

   C 85 and 80

   D 95 and 100

Use the box plots for 3 and 4.

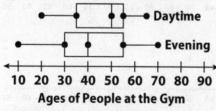

Ages of People at the Gym

3. Which value is greater for the people who go to the gym in the daytime than for the people who go in the evening?

   A range   C median

   B interquartile range D maximum

4. Which group has more people?

   A Daytime people

   B Evening people

   C They have the same number.

   D You cannot tell from the box plots.

5. A sample is being chosen for a survey to find out how people feel about adding more stop signs near a school. Which group would be **least** biased?

   A randomly chosen voters

   B randomly chosen drivers

   C randomly chosen students

   D randomly chosen teachers

6. A random sample of 60 was taken from a shipment of 12,500 light bulbs. There were 2 defective bulbs in the sample. How many defective bulbs would you expect in the entire shipment?

   A 250   C 2,500

   B 417   D 4,167

7. A toy company produces 1,000 toys per month. In January, 75 toys did not meet quality standards. The toy company generates a random sample to simulate 10 toys to inspect in February. The integers 1 to 75 represent toys that are below standard.

   726   687   329   68   134
   355   983   619   211   512

   Based on this sample, how many toys will not meet quality standards in February?

   A 1   C 10

   B 75   D 150

8. Which statement about the data is true?

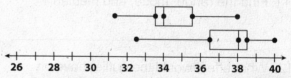

   A The difference between the medians is about 4 times the range.

   B The difference between the medians is about 4 times the IQR.

   C The difference between the medians is about 2 times the range.

   D The difference between the medians is about 2 times the IQR.

9. Each cell in the table represents the number of family members in one 15-block neighborhood. A real estate agent uses a random sample to estimate the average family size in the neighborhood.

⑥	1	3	4	6
5	6	⑤	④	8
⑦	③	4	7	5

The circled numbers represent the agent's random sample. Use the mean of the random sample to estimate the total number of people in the entire 15-block neighborhood.

_____

Use this random sample for 10–12.

Library Items Checked Out
2, 3, 13, 3, 2, 2, 3, 6, 1, 2, 6

10. Make a dot plot to display the data.

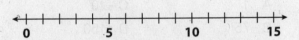

11. Find the range, mode, and median.

_____

12. What effect would the outlier have on the mean?

_____

_____

13. Tia wants to find out students' favorite after-school activity. She asks a sample of students, "Do you like doing sports after school?" Rewrite the question so it is not biased.

_____

_____

Use the two random samples for 14–16.

In-Store Purchases ($)
30, 34, 35, 37, 38, 46, 48, 52, 53, 56, 64, 64, 71, 80, 82

Online Purchases ($)
46, 50, 52, 52, 53, 58, 60, 61, 64, 65, 74, 75, 77, 80, 88

14. Use the two number lines below to make box plots to display each data set.

15. Find the medians and the ranges.

In-Store: _____

Online: _____

16. How would you compare these samples?

_____

_____

UNIT 5

Statistics

Unit Test: C

Use the dot plots for 1 and 2.

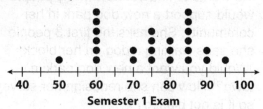

Semester 1 Exam

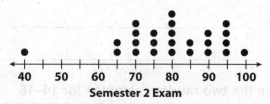

Semester 2 Exam

1. What are the means for the Semester 1 exam and the Semester 2 exam?

   A 75 and 79.8

   B 75 and 80

   C 85 and 80

   D 95 and 100

2. What is the difference in the medians of the two exams?

   A 5 points   C 15 points

   B 10 points   D no difference

Use the box plots for 3 and 4.

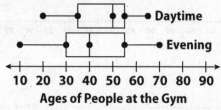

Ages of People at the Gym

3. What is the difference in the interquartile ranges of the two data sets?

   A 5 years   C 20 years

   B 10 years   D 25 years

4. Which group has a greater mean age?

   A Daytime people

   B Evening people

   C They means are the same.

   D You usually cannot find means from box plots.

5. A researcher used a sample median to estimate a population median. Then she decided her sample was biased. What can she conclude about the population median?

   A It is too small.

   B It is too large.

   C It is greater than the mean.

   D It may not represent the population.

6. What must a sample be to be useful in making predictions about the population?

   A large   C accurate

   B random   D representative

7. A toy company produces 1,250 toys per month. In January, 75 toys did not meet quality standards. The toy company generates a random sample to simulate 20 toys to inspect in February. The integers 1 to 75 represent toys that are below standard.

165	238	1066	1054	1103
1001	1248	607	699	403
944	229	1020	924	43
206	502	767	631	319

   Based on this sample, how many toys will not meet quality standards in February?

   A 1   C 75

   B 63   D 150

8. Which statement about the data is true?

City 1	City 2
65°, 68°, 63°, 55°, 59°, 78°, 70°, 75°, 72°, 75°, 71°, 68°	45°, 48°, 43°, 35°, 39°, 58°, 50°, 55°, 52°, 55°, 51°, 48°

   A The difference between the means is about 2 times the MAD.

   B The difference between the means is about 3 times the MAD.

   C The difference between the means is about 4 times the MAD.

   D The difference between the means is about 5 times the MAD.

9. Each cell in the table represents the average daily water usage in gallons by each house in one 15-block district of a town with 112 districts. A county agency uses a random sample to estimate the water usage of the entire town.

(601)	415	357	136	(525)
434	475	(352)	221	368
(324)	482	388	(415)	492

The circled numbers represent the random sample. What is the estimated daily water usage of the entire town?

_____

Use this random sample for 10–12.

Library Items Checked Out
7, 5, 2, 3, 13, 3, 2, 2, 3, 6, 1, 2, 6

10. Make a box plot to display the data.

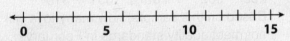

11. Find the mean with and without the outlier.

_____

12. Write a conclusion about the data.

_____

_____

13. Tia wants to find out how many people would support a new dog park in her community. She asks the first 3 people she sees walking a dog on her block, "Would you want a new dog park in town?" How can she redesign her survey so it is not biased?

_____

_____

Use the two random samples for 14–16.

In-Store Purchases ($)
37, 38, 30, 64, 80, 52, 56, 82, 71, 34, 46, 35, 48, 64, 53

Online Purchases ($)
52, 64, 77, 60, 50, 80, 75, 52, 58, 65, 88, 46, 53, 61, 74

14. Use the two number lines below to make box plots to display each data set.

30 35 40 45 50 55 60 65 70 75 80 85 90 95

30 35 40 45 50 55 60 65 70 75 80 85 90 95

15. Find the means.

In-Store:_____

Online:_____

16. What can you infer by comparing these samples?

_____

_____

UNIT 5

Statistics
Unit Test: D

Use the dot plots for 1 and 2.

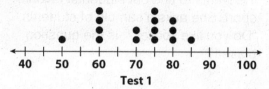

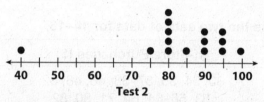

The dot plots show scores for 15 students on two tests.

1. Which test has an outlier?

   A   Test 1

   B   Test 2

   C   both tests

2. Which test has a greater median?

   A   Test 1

   B   Test 2

   C   They have the same median.

Use the box plots for 3 and 4.

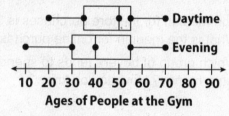

3. Which value is the same for both daytime and evening people at the gym?

   A   median age

   B   maximum age

   C   range of ages

4. Which statement **best** compares the two groups of people?

   A   The daytime people are older.

   B   The daytime people are younger.

   C   More people come in the daytime.

5. A survey will ask people if they want more stop signs near a school. Which group would probably be biased **against** this idea?

   A   students

   B   teachers

   C   drivers

6. There are 10,000 light bulbs in a shipment. In a sample of 100 bulbs, 5 were broken. How many broken bulbs would you expect in the whole shipment?

   A   5 bulbs

   B   50 bulbs

   C   500 bulbs

7. A toy company uses a random sample to simulate 10 toys to inspect out of a large group of toys. The integers 1 to 5 represent toys that are below standard.

76	68	32	2	14
35	93	61	21	51

   Based on this sample, how many toys will be below standard?

   A   1 out of 10

   B   1 out of 100

   C   1 out of 1000

8. Tara measured the heights of roses and sunflowers in her garden. Here are statistics on the data

   Roses:
   mean = 24 inches, range = 3 inches

   Sunflowers:
   mean = 36 inches, range = 3 inches

   Which statement about the data is true?

   A   The difference between the means is 2 times the range.

   B   The difference between the means is 3 times the range.

   C   The difference between the means is 4 times the range.

Statistics

9. The circled numbers represent a random sample of all the numbers in the table. By finding the mean of the circled numbers, you can estimate the mean of all the numbers.

⑥	1	3	4	6
5	6	⑤	④	8
⑦	③	4	7	5

What is the mean of the 5 circled numbers?

_____

Use the data set for 10–12.

Library Items Checked Out
2, 3, 13, 2, 3, 6, 2

The sample shows how many items 7 people checked out from a library.

10. Make a dot plot to show the data.

11. What is the range?

_____

12. What is the median?

_____

13. Tia wants to find out students' favorite sport. She asks a sample of students, "Do you like soccer?" Is the question biased?

_____

Use the two sets of data for 14–16.

In-Store Purchases ($)
30, 34, 35, 37, 38, 46, 48, 52, 53, 56, 64, 64, 71, 80, 82

Online Purchases ($)
46, 50, 52, 52, 53, 58, 60, 61, 64, 65, 74, 75, 77, 80, 88

14. The box plots below show the data sets. Finish the box plots by adding the whiskers.

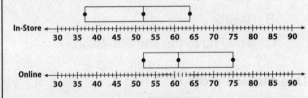

15. The median for in-store purchases is $52. What is the median for online purchases?

16. Which group of buyers tends to spend more money? How do you know?

_____

_____

UNIT 5

Statistics

Performance Task

When two number cubes are rolled, which sum is most likely? In this activity, you will generate a random sample to simulate sums of rolling the cubes.

You will Need
- 10 landline phone numbers with *the same* area code
- 10 cell phone numbers with *various* area codes
- Paper for making dot plots and box plots

---

1. This dot plot shows the possible sums when two number cubes are rolled. For example there are 3 different ways to get a sum of 4: (1, 3), (2, 2), and (3, 1).

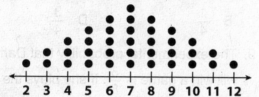

   On a separate sheet of paper, make a box plot for this data.

2. Use your calculator to simulate rolling the number cubes 18 times. For the simulated sample, use randInt(1, 6) and generate 18 pairs of numbers. Add each pair to represent the sum of a pair of rolled number cubes. Make a chart like the one below to record the sums.

Sum	2	3	4	5
Rolls				

3. On a separate sheet of paper, make a dot plot and a box plot to display the data from Exercise 2.

4. Why are your results different from the data display in Exercise 1?

   _____

   _____

   _____

Are the digits 0 through 9 equally distributed in phone numbers? You will analyze and compare landline and cell phone data in box plots and dot plots.

5. Imagine that the 10 digits in 10 phone numbers were equally distributed. A box plot for the data would look like this.

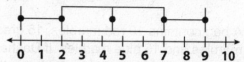

   Find the range, interquartile range, and median. (The median can be two numbers.)

   _____

   _____

6. On a separate sheet of paper, make a dot plot showing data in Exercise 5. What is the mean? _____

7. Use the landline phone numbers. On a separate sheet of paper, make a dot plot. Which digits appear most often? Why did this happen?

   _____

   _____

8. Use the cell phone numbers. On a separate sheet of paper, make a dot plot and a box plot.

9. Compare the cell phone box plot with the one from Exercise 5.

   _____

   _____

   _____

| UNIT | **Probability** |
| 6 | |

Unit Test: A

1. Kathleen rolled a number cube that has sides labeled 1 to 6. What is the probability that she rolled a 2 or a 4?

   A $\frac{1}{6}$ C $\frac{1}{2}$

   B $\frac{1}{3}$ D $\frac{3}{4}$

2. A bag contains 10 red marbles, 15 green marbles and 15 blue marbles. If Dashawn draws a marble from the bag, what is the probability that it is a red marble?

   A $\frac{1}{4}$ C $\frac{1}{2}$

   B $\frac{1}{3}$ D $\frac{2}{3}$

3. Kendra flips a coin 3 times. What is the probability that she flips tails all 3 times?

   A $\frac{1}{8}$ C $\frac{2}{3}$

   B $\frac{3}{8}$ D $\frac{7}{8}$

4. The probability that John receives junk mail is 11 percent. If he receives 94 pieces of mail in a week, about how many of them can he expect to be junk mail?

   A 5   C 15

   B 10   D 20

5. Gene made a two-digit code. The first digit is odd. How many possible codes can he choose from?

   A 5   C 50

   B 15   D 100

6. Aurelio can choose between 3 pairs of pants and 4 shirts. How many different outcomes are in the sample space?

   A 7   C 34

   B 12   D 81

7. A classroom has 7 blue chairs, 5 green chairs, 18 red chairs and 9 yellow chairs. If a chair is selected at random, which color is most likely to be chosen?

   A blue   C red

   B green   D yellow

8. Gisele spins a spinner that has equally sized yellow, green, blue and red sections. What is the probability that Gisele spins orange?

   A 0   C $\frac{1}{2}$

   B $\frac{1}{4}$ D $\frac{3}{4}$

9. The experimental probability that Daria will win a game is $\frac{3}{8}$. If she plays the game 80 times, how many times can she expect to win?

   A 10   C 30

   B 20   D 40

10. Jackson flipped a coin ten times. He flipped heads 4 times and tails 6 times. What is the experimental probability that Jackson will flip heads on his next flip?

    A $\frac{1}{6}$ C $\frac{1}{2}$

    B $\frac{2}{5}$ D $\frac{3}{4}$

11. Melissa rolls two number cubes, each with sides that are labeled 1 to 6. What is the probability that both number cubes show a 1?

    A $\frac{1}{6}$ C $\frac{1}{24}$

    B $\frac{1}{12}$ D $\frac{1}{36}$

12. A sandwich shop offers 3 types of bread and 4 types of meat. How many different sandwiches consisting of 1 type of bread and 1 type of meat are possible?

_____

13. The probability that Doreen wins a game of chance is $\frac{1}{3}$. Doreen plays the game 300 times, how many times can she expect to win the game?

_____

14. **Tyler's Survey Results**

		Eye Color	
		Brown	Blue
Hair Color	Brown	9	5
	Blonde	12	14

Tyler recorded the hair color and eye color of students walking in the hallway outside her homeroom. What is the experimental probability that the next student she sees will have blue eyes?

_____

15. Brianna rolls a number cube that has sides labeled 1 to 6 and flips a coin. Write the list of possible outcomes.

_____
_____
_____

16. Maria randomly selects a number from the list of numbers below.

56, 90, 88, 76, 12

What is the probability that she selects an even number?

_____

17. **Kelly's Experimental Outcomes**

Trial	Outcome
1	3, H
2	3, T
3	4, T
4	2, H
5	5, T

Kelly conducted an experiment. In each trial she flipped a coin and rolled a number cube that has sides labeled 1 to 6. The results are shown above. What is the experimental probability that her next flip will be tails?

_____

18. Colleen wrote each of the letters A through Z on a separate piece of paper and put them in a hat. If she randomly selects a piece of paper from the hat, what is the probability that the letter on the piece of paper will be a vowel (A, E, I, O or U)?

_____

19. Divya planted a garden with equal numbers of roses, daffodils, and tulips. If she randomly selects a flower, what is the probability that it is a lily?

_____

UNIT
6

Probability

Unit Test: B

1. Dhalia rolls a number cube that has sides labeled 1 to 6 and then flips a coin. What is the probability that she rolls an even number and flips heads?

   A $\dfrac{1}{8}$ C $\dfrac{1}{2}$

   B $\dfrac{1}{4}$ D $\dfrac{3}{4}$

2. There are 4 kings in a standard deck of 52 playing cards. If Taquasia selects a card at random, what is the probability that it is **not** a king?

   A $\dfrac{1}{52}$ C $\dfrac{1}{2}$

   B $\dfrac{1}{13}$ D $\dfrac{12}{13}$

3. The experimental probability that Josie's dad gets home from work between 5 P.M. and 6 P.M. is equal to $\dfrac{5}{8}$. About what percent of the time will Josie's dad get home from work between 5 P.M. and 6 P.M.?

   A 37.5%   C 62.5%

   B 58%   D 85%

4. The probability that Jenya receives spam e-mail is 4 percent. If she receives 520 e-mails in a week, about how many of them can she expect to be spam?

   A 18   C 25

   B 21   D 29

5. Vinay made a password that consists of 3 digits. None of the digits are the same. How many possible passwords did Vinay choose from?

   A 30   C 720

   B 100   D 1,000

6. The probability of an event is 0.001. Which of the following best describes the event?

   A The event will never occur.

   B There is a small chance that the event will occur.

   C The event is likely to occur.

   D The event will definitely occur.

7. Alexa spins a spinner that is divided into equally-sized red, green, and blue sections. What is the probability that Alexa spins orange?

   A 0   C $\dfrac{2}{3}$

   B $\dfrac{1}{3}$ D 1

8. The experimental probability that Pedro will hit a hole in one at the golf course is $\dfrac{2}{5}$. If Pedro goes golfing 40 times in a year, how many times can he expect to hit a hole in one?

   A 16   C 25

   B 24   D 40

9. Yaron has a box of pencils. 5 are green, 12 are brown, 6 are yellow, and 4 are blue. If he selects a pencil at random, which color pencil would he be **least** likely to select?

   A green   C yellow

   B brown   D blue

10. Wendy noticed that out of 345 cars that passed by her house 56 were SUVs. About how many SUVs could she expect to see pass by if 2,100 cars were to pass her house?

    A 200   C 400

    B 300   D 500

UNIT 6 **Probability**

11. Arabella's password consists of one letter followed by 2 digits. What is the probability of correctly guessing Arabella's password?

_____

12. Andrew has 45 rock songs, 82 dance songs and 65 rap songs on his play list. If his music player randomly selects a song, what is the probability that it is **not** a dance song?

_____

13. **Benny's Survey Results**

		Eye Color	
		Brown	**Blue**
Hair Color	**Brown**	56	61
	Blonde	14	26

Benny recorded the eye color and hair color of people walking in a shopping mall. Based on the results of his survey, what is the experimental probability that a person walking in the shopping mall has brown hair and blue eyes?

_____

14. What is the difference between experimental and theoretical probability?

_____

15. If Dennis rolls 2 number cubes with sides labeled 1 to 6, what is the probability that the sum of the numbers is greater than or equal to 10?

_____

16. If the probability of an event happening is p, what is an algebraic expression that represents the probability that the event does **not** happen?

_____

17. **Maurico's Marble Draws**

Color	Frequency
Red	12
Yellow	14
Blue	16
Green	18

Maurico conducted an experiment in which he drew marbles out of a bag and recorded the color. The results of the experiment are shown in the table above. What is the probability that Mauricio drew a yellow marble?

_____

18. Elizabeth wants to use a standard number cube to do a simulation for a scenario that involves three equal outcomes. What is one way in which she can do this?

_____

_____

19. Daniela flipped a coin and spun a spinner that is divided into four equal-size sectors colored red, yellow, green, and orange. Write the sample space of all the possible outcomes.

_____

_____

Probability

Unit Test: C

1. Li rolls a number cube that has sides labeled 1 to 6 and then flips a coin. What is the probability that she rolls an odd number and flips tails?

   A $\frac{1}{8}$ C $\frac{1}{2}$

   B $\frac{1}{4}$ D $\frac{3}{4}$

2. A bag contains 5 red marbles, 6 green marbles, and 3 blue marbles. If Cymra draws a marble, puts it back in the bag and then draws another marble, what is the probability that both marbles she draws will be red?

   A $\frac{5}{14} \times \frac{4}{13}$ C $\frac{5}{14} + \frac{4}{13}$

   B $\frac{5}{14} \times \frac{5}{14}$ D $\frac{5}{14} + \frac{5}{14}$

3. If Cole flips a coin three times, what is the probability that he will flip tails at least twice?

   A $\frac{1}{8}$ C $\frac{1}{2}$

   B $\frac{3}{8}$ D $\frac{7}{8}$

4. The probability that Linda receives spam e-mail is 4 percent. If she receives 520 e-mails in a week, about how many of them can she expect to be spam?

   A 18   C 25

   B 21   D 29

5. Morgan knows the probability of event A occurring is 0.56. What must be true about the probability that events A and B occur?

   A The probability is less than 0.56.

   B The probability is equal to 0.56.

   C The probability is greater than 0.56.

   D It is impossible to tell what the probability will be.

6. Shaul made a password that consists of one letter followed by two digits. The two digits are different. How many possible passwords did Shaul choose from?

   A 90   C 720

   B 260   D 2,340

7. Tomas spins a spinner that is divided into equally-sized sections that are shaded yellow, green, blue, and red. What is the probability that Tomas spins pink?

   A 0   C $\frac{1}{2}$

   B $\frac{1}{4}$ D $\frac{3}{4}$

8. The experimental probability that Ming will win a game of chance is $\frac{2}{5}$. The experimental probability that Tyrell will win the same game is $\frac{5}{8}$. If Ming and Tyrell each play 200 games, how many more games can Tyrell expect to win?

   A 16   C 25

   B 24   D 45

9. Desiree has a box of grease pencils. 8 are green, 10 are yellow, 9 are brown, and 5 are blue. If Desiree selects a grease pencil at random, which color is she twice as likely to select as blue?

   A green   C yellow

   B brown   D blue

10. Wendy noticed that out of 345 cars that passed by her house 56 were SUVs. About how many SUVs could she expect to see pass by if 2,100 cars were to pass her house?

    A 200   C 400

    B 300   D 500

UNIT 6 **Probability**

11. Arabella's password consists of 1 letter followed by 2 digits. What is the probability of correctly guessing Arabella's password?

_____

12. Ty's experimental probability of winning a certain game is $\frac{1}{3}$. Jana's experimental probability of winning the same game is $\frac{3}{4}$. If Ty and Jana each played the game 150 times, about how many more games would Jana expect to win?

_____

13. **Lydia's Survey Results**

		Favorite School Subject	
		English	Math
Favorite Sport	Football	34	15
	Baseball	32	41

Lydia recorded the favorite school subject and favorite sport for students in the school band. Based on the results of her survey, what is the experimental probability that the favorite school subject of a student surveyed is math?

_____

14. At the same time, Marisol rolls 2 number cubes that each have sides labeled 1 to 6. What is the probability that the product of the numbers will be greater than or equal to 24?

_____

15. Leni can choose between apple, orange and grapefruit juice. She can choose between the sizes small, medium and large. If she chooses a drink at random, what is the probability that she chooses orange juice in a medium size cup?

_____

16. **Deirdre's Experimental Outcomes**

Trial	Outcome
1	Red, H
2	Red, T
3	Blue, T
4	Green, H
5	Blue, T

Deirdre flipped a coin then spun a spinner 5 times. The results are shown in the table above. What is the experimental probability that Deirdre spun green?

_____

17. The experimental probability that Alexander wins a tennis match is 0.21. If he plays 40 tennis matches in the next week, about how many matches can Alexander expect to **lose**?

_____

18. Colin remembers nine digits of a ten-digit phone number. He remembers that the last digit is an even number. If he guesses the last digit, what is the probability that he dials the correct number?

_____

UNIT 6

Probability

Unit Test: D

1. A number cube has sides that are labeled 1 to 6. Jamal rolls the number cube. What is the probability that he will roll a 2?

   A $\frac{1}{8}$

   B $\frac{1}{6}$

   C $\frac{1}{3}$

2. A bag contains 10 red marbles and 15 green marbles. If Yuki selects a marble from the bag without looking, what is the probability that she will pull out a red marble?

   A $\frac{1}{5}$

   B $\frac{2}{5}$

   C $\frac{1}{2}$

3. Kendra flips a fair coin two times. What is the probability that she will flip tails both times?

   A $\frac{1}{8}$

   B $\frac{1}{4}$

   C $\frac{1}{2}$

4. The probability that Kimmy makes a basket is $\frac{7}{10}$. If she shoots 100 baskets, how many can she expect to make?

   A 7

   B 30

   C 70

5. A classroom has 14 blue chairs, 5 green chairs and 11 red chairs. If a chair is selected from the classroom at random, which color is most likely to be chosen?

   A blue

   B green

   C red

6. A spinner is divided into four equal-size sections that are numbered 1, 2, 3, and 4. Arlene spins the spinner. What is the probability that she spins 2?

   A 0

   B $\frac{1}{4}$

   C $\frac{1}{2}$

7. Ravi is shooting arrows at a target. The experimental probability that one will hit a bull's eye is $\frac{1}{2}$. If Ravi shoots 20 arrows, how many times can he expect to hit a bull's eye?

   A 0

   B 10

   C 20

8. Jackson flipped a coin 10 times. He flipped heads 3 times and tails 7 times. What is the experimental probability that Jackson will flip heads on his next flip?

   A $\frac{3}{10}$

   B $\frac{1}{2}$

   C $\frac{7}{10}$

UNIT 6

Probability

9. A sandwich shop offers two types of bread and five types of meat. How many different sandwiches that are made of one type of bread and one type of meat are possible?

_____

10. The probability that Teddy wins a certain game of chance is $\frac{1}{4}$. If Teddy plays the game 120 times, how many times can he expect to win the game?

_____

11.   **Lana's Survey Results**

		Eye Color	
		Brown	**Blue**
Gender	**Boy**	10	15
	Girl	15	20

Lana recorded the gender and eye color of students passing in the hallway at her school. What is the experimental probability that the next student she sees will be a boy with brown eyes?

_____

12. Andrew randomly selects a digit. What is the probability that the digit he selects is an even number?

_____

13. Mercedes can select from 2 types of apples and 3 types of pears. If she randomly selects 1 apple and 1 pear, how many possible choices does she have?

_____

14. Bo randomly selects a number from the list of numbers below.

0, 5, 10, 100

What is the probability that he selects a **negative** number?

_____

15.   **Luke's Experimental Outcomes**

Trial	Outcome
1	3, Heads
2	3, Heads
3	4, Tails
4	2, Heads
5	5, Tails

Luke conducted an experiment. In each trial, he rolled a number cube that has sides labeled 1 to 6 and then flipped a coin. The results are shown above. What is the experimental probability that his next flip will be heads?

_____

16. Felix randomly picked 12 flowers from a garden. Three of the flowers he picked were roses. What is the experimental probability that the next flower he picks will be a rose?

_____

17. Rajani planted an herb garden with equal numbers of rosemary, thyme, and sage plants. If she randomly selects a plant, what is the probability that it is a thyme plant?

_____

UNIT
6

Probability
Performance Task

1. A spinner is divided into 4 equal-size sections. The 4 sections are colored red, green, orange, and blue. If Ana spins the spinner twice, what are the possible outcomes?

   _____

   _____

   _____

2. If Ana spins the spinner once, what is the theoretical probability that she will spin green?

   _____

3. Ana spins the spinner 10 times. She spins green 4 times. What is the experimental probability that Ana will spin green on the next spin?

   _____

4. Why is your answer to Exercise 2 different from your answer to Exercise 3?

   _____

   _____

   _____

5. Use the theoretical probability. If Ana spins the spinner 400 times, how many times can she expect to spin green?

   _____

6. Ana wants to use a simulation to predict the number of times she will spin green. If she uses a random number generator and the digits 1 through 8, what is one way she can set up the simulation?

   _____

   _____

   _____

Benchmark Test: Modules 1–3

1. Which of the following numbers is **not** equivalent to $-\dfrac{15}{3}$?

   A $\dfrac{-15}{-3}$

   B $\dfrac{-15}{3}$

   C $\dfrac{15}{-3}$

   D -5

2. Mike scored –5 points on the first round and –8 on the second round. What was Mike's total score for the two rounds?

   A –13
   B –3
   C 3
   D 13

3. Four students put their game scores on the number line below. Which pair of students have a combined score of 0?

   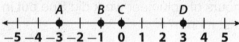

   A A and B
   B B and C
   C A and D
   D B and D

4. Jessica drank $\dfrac{1}{8}$ gallon of orange juice, and her brother Sam drank $\dfrac{1}{3}$ of the same gallon. How much of the gallon of orange juice did they drink?

   A $\dfrac{1}{11}$ gal

   B $\dfrac{2}{11}$ gal

   C $\dfrac{11}{24}$ gal

   D $\dfrac{15}{24}$ gal

5. A submarine changed its depth by –24 feet each minute for 6 minutes. What was the total change in depth at the end of the 6 minutes?

   A –144 ft
   B –30 ft
   C –4 ft
   D 30 ft

6. Inez has $2\dfrac{1}{4}$ pounds of potatoes. For the picnic, she needs $8\dfrac{1}{2}$ pounds of potatoes. How many more pounds of potatoes does Inez need to buy?

   A $5\dfrac{1}{4}$ lb

   B $5\dfrac{3}{4}$ lb

   C $6\dfrac{1}{4}$ lb

   D $10\dfrac{3}{4}$ lb

7. The temperature outside was 3°F at midnight. During the next hour the temperature fell 7°. What was the temperature at 1 A.M.?

   A –10°F
   B –4°F
   C 4°F
   D 10°F

8. Al's cat weighs $6\dfrac{3}{5}$ pounds. What is the weight of Al's cat written as a decimal?

   A 6.3 lb
   B 6.5 lb
   C 6.6 lb
   D 6.8 lb

9. A used car is on sale for $3,600. Eric offered the owner of the car $\dfrac{4}{5}$ of the asking price. How much was Eric's offer?

   A $1,440
   B $2,880
   C $3,240
   D $4,500

10. Reva is playing a bean-bag toss game. For each bag that misses the board, the player scores –8 points. Reva misses the board 4 times in one game. What is her total score for those 4 tosses?

    A –32 points
    B –4 points
    C –2 points
    D 12 points

Benchmark Test: Modules 1–3

11. What is the product of $(-2)(4)(-3)$?

   A −24   C 12

   B −12   D 24

12. One gallon of polyurethane covers 350 square feet. How many square feet will 2.5 gallons cover?

   A 352.5 ft^2

   B 700 ft^2

   C 875 ft^2

   D $1,050 \text{ ft}^2$

13. Alexandra ran $2\frac{7}{10}$ miles on Monday. She ran twice as far on Tuesday. How far did Alexandra run in all on those two days?

   A $6\frac{1}{10}$ mi   C $7\frac{7}{10}$ mi

   B $7\frac{1}{10}$ mi   D $8\frac{1}{10}$ mi

14. Jordan bought 9 pounds of fruit. He paid $2.39 a pound for 5 pounds. He paid $1.99 a pound for the rest. How much did Jordan spend on fruit?

   A $4.38   C $19.91

   B $13.94   D $39.12

15. In one game, teams of 4 players split their final scores evenly among team members. One team ended the game with a score of −24 points. How many points did each player receive?

   A −6   C −20

   B −8   D −96

16. What is the sum of the integers below?
   −9, 4, 10, −4, 8, −4

   A −5   C 10

   B 5   D 18

17. Which value is equal to $-18 \div (-9)$?

   A −2   C 0.2

   B −0.2   D 2

18. A football team lost 3 yards on one play and lost 6 yards on the next play. What was their total change in yardage in the two plays?

   A −18 yd   C −3 yd

   B −9 yd   D 18 yd

19. Sue volunteers at a hospital. Last month she volunteered $1\frac{3}{4}$ hours on each of 4 Saturdays. She also volunteered $\frac{3}{4}$ hour on 3 Wednesday evenings. How many hours of volunteer work did Sue put in last month?

   A 7 h   C $9\frac{1}{4}$ h

   B $7\frac{3}{4}$ h   D $12\frac{1}{4}$ h

20. On Monday morning, Raj had $225 in his checking account. The table shows activity in the account for the next four days. What was the balance in Raj's checking account on Friday?

Day	Deposit	Withdrawal
Monday	none	$27.25
Tuesday	$75.50	none
Wednesday	$32.19	$61.95
Thursday	none	$14.21

   A $103.41   C $332.28

   B $229.28   D $436.41

Benchmark Test: Modules 1–3

21. Which problem could be solved with division?

   A   Steven has $\frac{1}{4}$ yard of felt. He needs $2\frac{1}{2}$ yards of felt. How much more felt does he need?

   B   Steven has $\frac{1}{2}$ yard of felt. He needs $\frac{1}{4}$ yard for each flag. How many flags can he make?

   C   Steven has $\frac{1}{2}$ yard of felt. He uses $\frac{1}{4}$ of the felt for each flag. How much felt will he use on each flag?

   D   Steven has $\frac{1}{2}$ yard of felt. He used $\frac{1}{4}$ yard to make a flag. How much felt does he have left?

22. In a card game, a player draws 2 cards. The player finds the product of the integers shown on the pair of cards to find how many points are scored for that round.

   Carlotta drew the two cards shown below.

   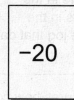

   How many points does Carlotta score for this round?

   A −100   C 4

   B −25   D 100

23. Carlos showed a problem on a number line.

   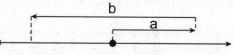

   Which of the following is **not** shown by Carlos' drawing?

   A $a + (-b)$

   B $a - (-b)$

   C $a - b$

   D $|a| - |b|$

24. Christopher earned $153.20. He saved $34.50. He spent the rest on 2 new pair of shoes. How much did Christopher spend on new shoes?

   A $59.35   C $129.30

   B $118.70   D $187.70

25. Destiny bought $10\frac{1}{2}$ yards of material for costumes for the city pageant. She will use $1\frac{1}{4}$ yards of the material to make each costume. How many costumes can Destiny complete?

   A 8   C 9

   B $8\frac{4}{10}$ D $9\frac{1}{4}$

26. The superspeedway at Daytona International Speedway is 2.5 miles long. The road course there is 1.4 times as long as the superspeedway. How long is the road course?

   A 1.1 mi

   B 1.8 mi

   C 3.5 mi

   D 3.9 mi

Benchmark Test: Modules 1–3

27. Four students put their game scores on the number line below. Which pair of students have a combined score of 0?

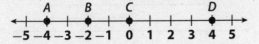

_____

28. On the school trip, Margie spent $12.40 on 2 souvenirs. Each souvenir cost the same amount. The amount of tax was $0.72. How much did each souvenir cost?

_____

29. The lowest elevation in Louisiana is −68 feet. The lowest elevation in California is 214 feet lower than the lowest elevation in Louisiana. What is the lowest elevation in California?

_____

30. Last week Marcella earned $432. During that week, she worked 8 hours for 4 days and 4 hours on 1 day. What was Marcella's pay per hour?

_____

31. Sierra collected 39 seashells before breakfast and $2\frac{1}{3}$ times as many after breakfast. How many seashells did Sierra collect in all?

_____

32. One machine's value changed by −$6,400 over 5 years. The company charges off such changes in value as depreciation. Each year an equal amount is charged off. What was the change in value that would be charged off each year for this machine?

_____

33. A diver descended 60 feet in 3 minutes. What was the diver's change in depth per minute?

_____

34. Find the difference between −34 and −43.

_____

35. What is −64.4 ÷ (−3.22)?

_____

36. The highest elevation in Minnesota is about 700 meters above sea level. That is $6\frac{2}{3}$ times higher than the highest elevation in Florida. To the nearest meter, what is the highest elevation in Florida?

_____

37. Jenna has 3.375 yards of rope. Write 3.375 as a fraction in simplest form.

_____

38. Dylan walked $5\frac{3}{5}$ miles. What is $5\frac{3}{5}$ written as a decimal?

_____

39. Haley jogged 1.5 kilometers in the morning and 2.8 kilometers in the afternoon. How far did she jog that day?

_____

40. The wind-chill factor measures how cold it feels based on both temperature and wind speed. The wind-chill factor was 8°F at 6 P.M. and dropped to −8°F by 10 P.M. What was the change in the wind-chill factor between 6 P.M. and 10 P.M.?

_____

Mid-Year Test Modules 4–7

1. Zachary spent $61.50 for 15 gallons of premium gasoline. What was the price per gallon?

   A $0.41   C $4.10

   B $1.41   D $6.15

2. Mikela earned $65.25 for 9 hours of work. This week she earned $101.50 for 14 hours. Which equation represents the relationship between the hours worked, x, and Mikela's pay, y?

   A $y = 7.25x$ C $y = 14x$

   B $y = 9x$ D $y = 23x$

3. A bank pays 3% annual simple interest on CDs (certificates of deposit) of $25,000. The Branson family invests in 3 of the $25,000 CDs. How much interest does the family make in one year?

   A $22.50   C $2,250.00

   B $225.00   D $22,500.00

4. The water level in the tank changes by x inches every hour. In 4 hours, the tank's water level decreased at least 22 inches. Sue wrote $4x \geq 22$. What is the solution to the inequality?

   A $x > 5.5$ C $x \leq 5.5$

   B $x \geq 5.5$ D $x < 5.5$

5. A softball player gets a hit 22% of the times she is at bat. In 50 times at bat, about how many hits will the player get?

   A 11 times   C 33 times

   B 22 times   D 44 times

6. A 12-pack of boxes of raisins costs $4.86. Each box contains 1.5 ounces of raisins. To the nearest cent, what is the unit price of raisins per ounce?

   A $0.13/oz

   B $0.27/oz

   C $0.41/oz

   D $3.24/oz

7. Simplify $0.3(x - 2y) + 0.5x - y$.

   A $0.8x - 3y$ C $0.8x - y$

   B $0.8x - 1.6y$ D $0.8x + 0.4y$

8. A snack box contains at most 7 ounces of cheese. Fiona says the amount of cheese can be represented by $2x - 3$. Which graph shows the possible amount of cheese in the box?

   A

   B

   C

   D

9. A magazine has 172,500 subscribers. The records of the magazine show that each year 12% of readers fail to renew subscriptions. How many readers can the magazine expect to lose this year?

   A 870 subscribers

   B 17,250 subscribers

   C 20,700 subscribers

   D 36,792 subscribers

10. A truck travels 312 miles in 6.5 hours. What is the truck's speed for that trip?

    A 4.8 mi/h   C 50.2 mi/h

    B 48 mi/h   D 58 mi/h

11. Jakob is tiling a newly finished room. He estimates that he tiles about 9 square feet every $\dfrac{3}{4}$ hour. About how many square feet can he tile per hour?

    A 7 ft^2/h   C 12 ft^2/h

    B 10 ft^2/h   D 36 ft^2/h

12. Mittens are marked down 25%. The sale price is $3.15 a pair. What was the original price of a pair of mittens?

    A $3.40   C $4.20

    B $3.94   D $7.88

Name _____ Date _____ Class_____

Mid-Year Test Modules 4–7

13. Arturo's gym membership costs $100 per year plus $20 per month. Which equation represents the cost of membership for x months?

   A $y = 0.2x + 100$

   B $y = 2x + 100$

   C $y = 20x + 100$

   D $y = 100x + 20$

14. Which graph represents the relationship shown below?

$$y = 4x$$

A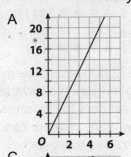
B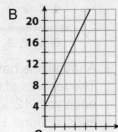
C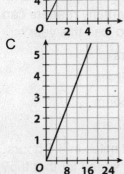
D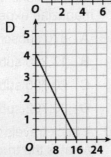

15. Historically, a college accepts about 15% of applicants. This year 4,880 students applied. About how many will be accepted?

   A 683 students

   B 732 students

   C 4,148 students

   D 5,612 students

16. At his job Lee earns $400 per week plus a 6% commission on his sales s. He wants to earn at least $550 this week. Which of the following represents this situation?

   A $400 + 0.06s = 550$

   B $400 + 0.06s \neq 550$

   C $400 + 0.06s \leq 550$

   D $400 + 0.06s \geq 550$

17. At the museum, you can buy 3 post cards for $5.40, 6 post cards for $10.80, or 9 post cards for $16.20. What is the constant of proportionality for buying post cards?

   A 1.60   C 2.70

   B 1.80   D 3.00

18. At her job Mila earns $\$x$ per month plus a bonus if her sales are over $5,000. Her bonus is 6% of her salary. Which is **not** a way to express Mila's monthly salary when her sales are over $5,000?

   A $x + 0.6x$

   B 106% of x

   C $x + 0.06x$

   D $1.06x$

19. Which expression is equal to 0 when simplified?

   A $2n - 3m - (2n + 3m)$

   B $6(x - y) + 2(3x + 3y)$

   C $15p - 15p \div 3$

   D $4a(2 - 3) + 4a$

20. Keighlee has at most 60 minutes to finish her homework. She knows math will take 20 minutes. The rest of the time she will spend writing the final version of her science report. She knows it takes 8 minutes to write each page. Which graph shows the possible number pages she can write?

21. Which of the following values is a solution to the equation below?

$$5p - 20 = 35$$

   A −11   C 3

   B −3   D 11

Mid-Year Test Modules 4–7

22. Which graph represents a proportional relationship?

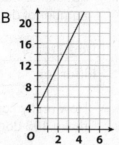

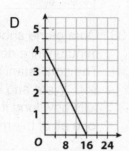

23. A museum has 639 pieces of African art in its collection. This is 55 fewer pieces of art than one-third of the art pieces the museum has from Europe. Which equation can you use to find n, the number of European art works in the museum's collection?

   A $\frac{1}{3}n - 55 = 639$

   B $\frac{1}{3}n + 55 = 639$

   C $3n - 55 = 639$

   D $3n + 55 = 639$

24. Which inequality is represented by the number line below?

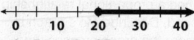

   A $5x - 15 \le 85$

   B $5x + 15 \le 85$

   C $5x - 15 \ge 85$

   D $5x + 85 \ge 15$

25. A pet store has 15 puppies, 12 kittens, and 6 rabbits. Which animals are in a ratio of 5:2?

   A puppies to kittens

   B kittens to rabbits

   C puppies to rabbits

   D kittens to puppies

26. Which shows the solution to the inequality

$$-4x > 36$$

   A $x > -9$ C $x < 9$

   B $x > 9$ D $x < -9$

27. Misha has $20 to spend at a book fair. The admission is $5 and each new paperback is $2.00. Which inequality expresses the number of new paperbacks that Misha can buy?

   A $2p - 5 \ge 20$

   B $2p + 5 \le 20$

   C $5p - 2 \le 20$

   D $5p + 2 \le 20$

28. A builder got an 8% bonus for finishing the project ahead of schedule. Which is one way to express how much the builder earned if d was the original amount the builder was to be paid?

   A $0.92d$ C $d + 0.08d$

   B $d + 800$ D $d + 0.8d$

29. Which is the solution to the inequality below?

$$-5n - 10 \ge 20$$

   A $n \le -2$

   B $n \ge -2$

   C $n \le -6$

   D $n \ge -6$

Mid-Year Test Modules 4–7

30. A car rental company charges $29.95 a day plus $0.40 per mile. How much will a two-day rental and 185 miles cost?

_____

31. An animal clinic charges $40 for vaccinations of kittens and $55 for vaccinations of puppies. Last week, the clinic earned $1,450 from vaccinations, including 14 puppies. How many kittens were vaccinated at the clinic last week?

_____

32. Josh simplified $4x - 8x \div 2$ and said the answer was $-2x$. What was Josh's error? What should his answer have been?

_____

_____

33. Tom's Sporting Goods pays $37 each for a certain brand of basketball. Tom marks up the price by 45%. To the nearest cent, what is the retail price in dollars of each basketball?

_____

34. Trey reads 10 pages in 25 minutes. At this rate, how many pages will he read in 45 minutes?

_____

35. Julianna wrote $-16 + x = -8$ on the board. Do not solve. Tell how you would simplify Julianna's expression.

_____

36. Crunchee Corporation increases the size of its granola packages from 16 ounces to 20 ounces. What is the percent of increase in the size of Crunchee's granola packages?

_____

37. The table shows the amount of flour needed to make dough for a certain number of dog treats.

Dog Treats	30	45	105
Flour (c)	2	3	?

How many cups of flour does it take to make 105 dog treats?

_____

38. On a game show, a contestant lost $2 a minute while doing a complicated task. The contestant can lose no more than $50. Write and solve an inequality that tells how long it takes for a contestant to lose all of the money.

_____

39. The price of a share of stock increases $45.69 over 3 days. What was the average rate of change in its price in dollars per day?

_____

40. Alicia says that in 8 years twice her dog's age will be 20. How old is Alicia's dog now? Write and solve an equation to solve the problem.

_____

41. Mo graphed a proportional relationship about speed. Describe Mo's graph by telling where the graph crosses the x-axis, where the graph crosses the y-axis, and whether the line of the graph is straight, curved, or broken.

_____

Benchmark Test Modules 8–11

Use the figure for 1–2.

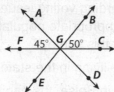

1. What is the measure of ∠CGD?

   A 45°   C 60°

   B 50°   D 85°

2. What is the measure of ∠EGD?

   A 50°   C 90°

   B 85°   D 95°

3. The scale in a drawing is 2 in.:8 ft. On the drawing, a room is $3\frac{1}{2}$ inches long. What is the length in feet of the actual room?

   A 8 ft   C 28 ft

   B 14 ft   D 56 ft

Use the figure for 4–7.

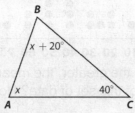

4. What is the value of x?

   A 30°   C 70°

   B 60°   D 80°

5. What is the measure of ∠ABC?

   A 50°   C 70°

   B 60°   D 80°

6. Suppose you double the size of ∠ACB. Now what is the measure of ∠BAC?

   A 40°   C 60°

   B 50°   D 100°

7. Suppose you cut the size of ∠ACB in half. Now what is the measure of ∠ABC?

   A 50°   C 90°

   B 70°   D 120°

Use the box plots for 8–9.

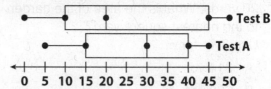

The plots represent the results of the last two tests taken byJoleen's math class. Each test had 50 questions.

8. Which test has the greater median? Find the difference between the medians.

   A Test A, 10   C Test A, 5

   B Test B, 10   D Test B, 5

9. Which test has the greater range? What is the difference between the ranges?

   A Test A, 25   C Test A, 10

   B Test B, 10   D Test B, 5

10. Brad cuts a triangular prism with a plane parallel to the base of the prism. What will the shape of the cross-section be?

    A a triangle smaller than the base

    B a triangle congruent to the base

    C a triangle larger than the base

    D a rectangle

11. In a random survey of 100 students, 30 chose soccer as their favorite sport to participate in. There are 350 students in the school. How many students are likely to choose soccer as their favorite sport to participate in?

    A 70   C 105

    B 95   D 117

12. The radius of a circular box is 21 centimeters. What is the circumference of the box? Use $\frac{22}{7}$ for π.

    A 66 cm

    B 132 cm

    C 176 cm

    D 1,386 cm

Benchmark Test Modules 8–11

13. A circular garden has a diameter of 20 yards. What is the area of the garden to the nearest square yard? Use 3.14 for π.

A 314 yd^2

B 628 yd^2

C 1,256 yd^2

D 3,140 yd^2

14. The circumference of the wheel on Beyoncé's bicycle is 63 inches. What is the diameter of the bicycle wheel to the nearest inch? Use 3.14 for π.

A 12 in.   C 20 in.

B 18 in.   D 32 in.

15. What is the area of the figure to the nearest square centimeter? It is composed of a symmetric hexagon and a semicircle.

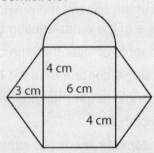

A 50 cm^2 C 100 cm^2

B 86 cm^2 D 129 cm^2

16. In an isosceles triangle the measure of the angle formed by the two congruent sides is 80°. What is the measure of each base angle?

A 40°   C 80°

B 50°   D 85°

17. What is the volume of the prism to the nearest tenth of an inch?

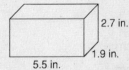

A 10.1 in^3 C 28.2 in^3

B 20.2 in^3 D 56.4 in^3

18. A newspaper is surveying voters from Idaho regarding voting issues. Which is the most appropriate population to sample for this survey?

A people living in the state of Idaho

B voters in Boise, the capital of Idaho

C people of voting age in the U.S.

D voters living in the state of Idaho

19. A map has the scale of 1 in.:50 mi. On the map, two cities are 4.5 inches apart. What is the actual distance between cities?

A 45 mi   C 225 mi

B 90 mi   D 450 mi

Use the dot plot for 20–21.

Number of Pages Assigned Each Day This Month in English Class

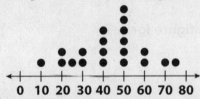

20. Which is the greater, the mean or the median of this set of data? How much greater?

A mean, 2 pages   C median, 2 pages

B mean, 5 pages   D median, 5 pages

21. What does the mode of this set of data represent?

A the number of days on which 50 pages of reading were assigned

B 50 percent of days on which a reading assignment was given

C the greatest number of pages assigned in English this month

D the most common reading assignment this month

Benchmark Test Modules 8–11

Use the prism for 22–23.

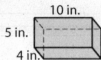

10 in.
5 in.
4 in.

22. What is the surface area of the prism?

   A 90 in^2 C 200 in^2

   B 110 in^2 D 220 in^2

23. What is the volume of the prism?

   A 90 in^3 C 200 in^3

   B 110 in^3 D 220 in^3

24. A circular rug has a diameter of 6 feet. To the nearest foot, what is the rug's area? Use 3.14 for π.

   A 19 ft^2 C 37 ft^2

   B 28 ft^2 D 113 ft^2

Use the box plots for 25–26.

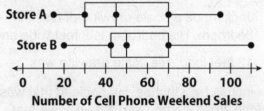

Store A
Store B
0   20   40   60   80   100
Number of Cell Phone Weekend Sales

25. What is the difference in medians of sales during the weekend?

   A 5   B 10   C 15   D 20

26. What is the difference in range of sales during the weekend?

   A 0   B 5   C 10   D 15

27. In a random survey of 50 students at Ryland Middle School, 32 said chocolate was their favorite flavor of yogurt. The school has 450 students. How many of them are likely to select chocolate as their favorite flavor?

   A 144 students   C 225 students

   B 162 students   D 288 students

28. The net below forms a rectangular prism. What is the total surface area of the prism?

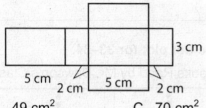

3 cm
5 cm 2 cm 5 cm 2 cm

   A 49 cm^2 C 70 cm^2

   B 62 cm^2 D 98 cm^2

29. Which of the following is a random sample of new car owners?

   A Pollsters randomly selecting new owner names from customer purchase lists to survey.

   B A car dealership representative talks to purchasers of new cars.

   C Owners of new cars are surveyed as they leave a fast-food restaurant.

   D Owners of hybrid cars are surveyed at gas stations.

30. Jeremiah wants to make a triangle from the three sticks below. What kind of triangle will he make?

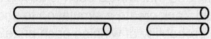

   A a scalene triangle

   B an equilateral triangle

   C an isosceles triangle

   D he cannot make a triangle

31. A grocer took a random survey of 40 customers. Twelve customers would like the store to stay open later. Suppose the grocer surveyed 100 more customers. How many of those 100 customers would likely want the store to stay open later?

   A 24   C 36

   B 30   D 70

Benchmark Test Modules 8–11

32. A wheel has a diameter of 15 inches. To the nearest inch, how many inches is its circumference? Use 3.14 for π.

_____

Use the dot plot for 33–34.

Books Read by Mr. Dawson's Class

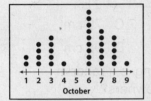 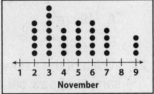

October   November

33. During which month was the median number of books read greater?

_____

34. During which month are the median and the mode the same?

_____

35. At the Pebble Pick at a school carnival the probability of drawing a pebble that wins a pencil is 50%, that wins a CD is 25%, and that wins a book is 25%. How could Zack create a simulation to show the probability of winning each prize?

_____

_____

36. To the nearest tenth, how many square units is the area of the figure below? It is composed of a trapezoid and a semicircle. Use 3.14 for π.

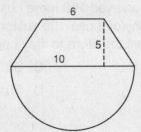

Use the figure for 37–38.

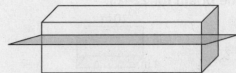

37. Yvette had a solid block of wood in the shape of a rectangular prism. She sawed the wood into two pieces by cutting on a line parallel to the base and perpendicular to the side. What will be the shape of the new base of each piece of wood?

_____

38. In relation to size, compare the size of the base of the original block of wood and the base of each new piece of wood.

_____

39. Jack made a scale drawing of his bedroom. His bedroom is 9 feet wide and 12 feet long. His scale drawing was $2\frac{1}{4}$ inches by 3 inches. He decided that was too small, so he used a new scale that was 3 times larger than the original scale. What is the new scale he used?

_____

40. Luanne has 3 straws. One straw is 6 in. long. The other two straws are 10 in. long. Make a sketch of the triangle Luanne can make from the straws. Tell what kind of triangle you made.

_____

End-of-Year Test

1. At 6 A.M. the temperature was –8°C. At noon the temperature was 3°C. What was the change of temperature between 6 A.M. and noon?

   A –11°C   C 5°C

   B –5°C   D 11°C

2. What is the quotient of $-18 \div \left(-\dfrac{1}{6}\right)$?

   A –108   C 3

   B –3   D 108

3. What is true about the relationship between miles and gallons?

gallons	2	5	6	9
miles	46	115	138	207

   A There is no relationship between miles and gallons.

   B There is a proportional relationship between miles and gallons.

   C There is a 1 to 23 relationship between miles and gallons.

   D There is a 20 to 1 relationship between miles and gallons.

4. Which decimal is equivalent to $\dfrac{7}{20}$?

   A 0.35   C 2.85

   B 1.34   D 7.20

5. At the farmers' market, you can buy 3 melons for $10.50, 6 melons for $21, or 9 melons for $31.50. What is the constant of proportionality for buying melons?

   A 3.50   C 10.50

   B 5.75   D 63.00

6. Jen makes necklaces by stringing different color beads. Each necklace is 18 inches long. Jen has an 86-inch length of beaded string. How many necklaces can she make?

   A 4   C 7

   B 5   D 8

7. The ground temperature at ABC airport is 5°F. For every 500 feet gained in altitude, the temperature outside the plane drops 1.6°F. At an altitude of 3,000 feet, what will be the likely outside temperature?

   A –9.6°F   C –3.4°F

   B –4.6°F   D 4.6°F

8. Terry skated 2 miles in $\dfrac{1}{2}$ hour. Which of the following represents the unit rate that Terry skates?

   A $\dfrac{1}{2}$ mi/h   C $\left(\dfrac{1}{2} \div 2\right)$ mi/h

   B $\left(2 \div \dfrac{1}{2}\right)$ mi/h   D 2 mi/h

9. Simplify $\dfrac{1}{2}(4a + b) - \dfrac{1}{4}(4a + b)$.

   A a C $2a + \dfrac{1}{4}b$

   B $a + \dfrac{1}{4}b$ D $2a - b$

10. Four croissants cost $2.60. How much will it cost to purchase 7 croissants?

    A $4.55   C $9.60

    B $5.20   D $10.77

11. A photo of a painting measures 13 inches by 17 inches. The scale factor is $\dfrac{1}{3}$. What size is the painting?

    A 4.3 in. × 5.7 in.

    B 26 in. × 34 in.

    C 39 in. × 51 in.

    D 65 in. × 85 in.

12. Which fraction is equivalent to –0.06?

    A $-\dfrac{1}{6}$ C $-\dfrac{7}{10}$

    B $-\dfrac{3}{5}$ D $-\dfrac{3}{50}$

End-of-Year Test

13. The cost of 50 pounds of pet food is $117.50. What is the cost for one pound of pet food?

 A $0.43   C $23.00

 B $2.35   D $235.00

14. On a map, the distance between two cities is 7.3 centimeters. The map scale is 1 cm:50 km. What is the actual distance between the two cities?

 A 365 cm   C 400 km

 B 365 km   D 500 km

15. Dallas got a raise. His hourly wage was increased from $9 to $10.25? What was the percent increase in Dallas's wage to the nearest whole percent?

 A 10%   C 14%

 B 12%   D 125%

16. What is the volume of the rectangular prism to the nearest cubic centimeter?

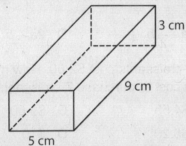

 A 68 cm^3 C 81 cm^3

 B 75 cm^3 D 135 cm^3

17. The experimental probability of seeing a hawk at the Avian Viewing Center on any given day is 20%. If Jun visits the center 240 days, on about how many days can she expect to see a hawk?

 A 24 days   C 96 days

 B 48 days   D 192 days

18. The circumference of a circle is 28π meters. What is its radius?

 A 7 m   C 21 m

 B 14 m   D 28 m

19. The graph shows the relationship between fees charged for downloading songs from a website and the number of songs downloaded. Which equation represents the relationship?

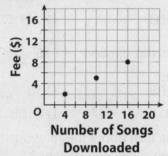

 A $y = 0.25x$ C $y = 0.75x$

 B $y = 0.50x$ D $y = 5x$

20. Based on the net shown below, what is the surface area of the pyramid to the nearest square inch?

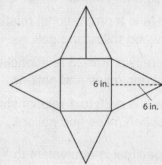

 A 63 in^2 C 81 in^2

 B 72 in^2 D 108 in^2

21. Zack flips a coin and rolls a number cube with sides labeled 1 to 6. What is the probability that he gets heads and a number greater than 4?

 A $\frac{1}{6}$ B $\frac{1}{4}$ C $\frac{1}{3}$ D $\frac{1}{2}$

22. The Healey family drove 192 miles in 4.5 hours. How many miles could they drive at this rate in 3 hours?

 A 64 mi   C 128 mi

 B 77 mi   D 184 mi

End-of-Year Test

23. Your school is choosing new school colors. Which group should you ask to get a random sample of student opinion?

    A ten 7th grade students

    B every tenth student that enters the building in the morning

    C twenty 1st and 2nd graders

    D every other student going into the principal's office

24. A rectangle is 8 inches long and 4 inches wide. A similar rectangle is 12 inches long. What is the width of the second rectangle to the nearest inch?

    A 4 in.   C 8 in.

    B 6 in.   D 10 in.

25. There are 25 counters in a bag: 6 red, 4 white, 7 blue, and 8 yellow. You choose one counter at random. Which color are you **least** likely to choose?

    A white   C blue

    B red   D yellow

26. Which table represents the same linear relationship as the equation $y = 3x + 5$?

    A
x	0	1	2	5
y	0	11	14	17

    B
x	2	3	4	5
y	1	4	7	10

    C
x	2	3	4	5
y	11	14	17	20

    D
x	2	3	4	5
y	15	20	25	30

27. Mae's cat weighs $5\frac{3}{8}$ pounds. What is this weight written as a decimal?

    A 5.125 lb   C 5.385 lb

    B 5.375 lb   D 5.625 lb

28. The sections of spinner below are shaded red, blue, or green. What is the probability that the spinner will land on blue **or** green?

    A $\frac{1}{3}$ C $\frac{2}{3}$

    B $\frac{1}{2}$ D $\frac{5}{8}$

29. Based on the dot plots below, which of the following is a true statement?

    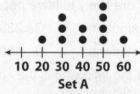

    Set A

    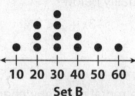

    Set B

    A Set B has the greater mode.

    B Set A has the lesser mean.

    C Set A is more symmetric than set B.

    D Set B has the greater range.

30. A diner has a breakfast special. A customer can chose scrambled, fried, or poached eggs. The breakfast comes with a side of bacon, sausage, or fruit salad. The customer can choose coffee, tea, or milk. You make a sample space of all the possible combinations. How many different combinations of eggs, side, and drink does a customer have to choose from?

    A 9   C 27

    B 12   D 135

End-of-Year Test

31. The net below is of a triangular prism. What is the surface area of the prism?

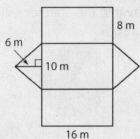

8 m
6 m
10 m
16 m

A   288 m²   C   318 m²

B   300 m²   D   476 m²

32. A school has 520 students. Dan surveys a random sample of 50 students and finds that 32 have pet cats. How many students are likely to have pet cats?

A   180 students   C   333 students

B   320 students   D   488 students

33. Which of the following is the solution for the inequality below?

$$-3x + 2 < 8$$

A $x > -3$ C $x < -2$

B $x > -2$ D $x < -3$

34. A bicycle rental company charges a $12 fee plus $3 per hour. Which equation represents this linear relationship?

A $y = 12x - 3$ C $y = 3x - 12$

B $y = 12x + 3$ D $y = 3x + 12$

35. To the nearest tenth, what is the area of the figure below? Use 3.14 for π.

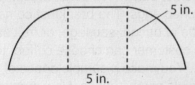

5 in.
5 in.

A   12.5 in²   C   37.5 in²

B   25.0 in²   D   64.3 in²

36. What is the measure of $\angle BGC$?

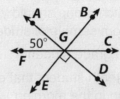

A   30°   C   45°

B   40°   D   50°

37. The Grabo family's monthly budget is shown in the circle graph. The family has a monthly income of $5,000. How much money do they spend on housing each month?

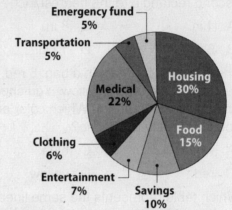

Emergency fund 5%
Transportation 5%
Medical 22%
Housing 30%
Clothing 6%
Food 15%
Entertainment 7%
Savings 10%

A $250   C $1,100

B $500   D $1,500

38. A storage trunk is 36 inches wide, 22 inches deep, and 44 inches high. What is the volume of the trunk to the nearest cubic inch?

A   4,356 in³   C   34,848 in³

B   17,4424 in³   D   46,656 in³

39. A circle has a radius of 9 inches. What is the area of the circle?

A   28.26 in²

B   56.52 in²

C   127.14 in²

D   254.34 in²

End-of-Year Test

40. The circle graph shows the results of an employment survey of 800 people. How many of the people surveyed were employed full time?

A 80 people   C 320 people

B 200 people   D 480 people

41. Which of the following is a random sample?

A Members of a polling organization survey city voters about who they expect to be elected mayor.

B A survey company asks 100 members at a concert who their favorite singer is.

C Customers at a pizza shop are surveyed about their favorite food.

D Carlos uses an e-mail survey to find out how many students have computers at home.

42. A 10-inch piece of ribbon is 25.4 centimeters long. How long will a 36-inch piece of ribbon be to the nearest hundredth of a centimeter?

A 14.17 cm   C 141.73 cm

B 91.44 cm   D 914.40 cm

43. One circle has a diameter of 10 inches. A second circle has a diameter that is twice the diameter of the first circle. What is the ratio of the area of the smaller circle to the larger circle?

A 1:2   B 1:3.14   C 1:4   D 1:8

Use the box plot for 44–45.

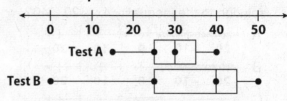

44. What is the difference between the medians for Test A and Test B?

A 10   C 20

B 15   D 30

45. Which statement is true based on the box plots?

A Test A had the greater range of scores.

B More students did better on Test A than on Test B.

C The interquartile range for Test B is greater than for Test A.

D One half of the students on each test got 25 or fewer questions correct.

Use the figure for 46–47.

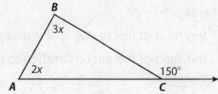

46. What is the measure of $\angle BAC$?

A 30°   C 60°

B 45°   D 75°

47. Which of the following is **not** true?

A $2x + 3x = 150$ C $3x - 2x = 30$

B $2x + 3x + 30 = 180$ D $2x + 3x \geq 180$

48. Which equation represents the data shown in the table below?

Cost (y)	5	10	15	20
Gallon (x)	2	4	6	8

A $y = 2x + 1$ C $y = 2.5x$

B $y = 3x - 1$ D $y = 2.5x + 1$

End-of-Year Test

49. Which number line represents the solution to the inequality $4x + 20 < 40$?

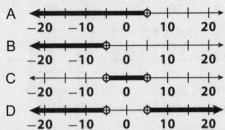

50. Three stores have the same mp3 player for sale. The regular price of the player is $50. Store A is offering the player on sale at 15% off the regular price. Store B is offering a $10 coupon to be deducted from the regular price. Store C is offering a rebate of $7.50 to purchasers. Which store is offering the mp3 player at the lowest cost?

    A   Store A

    B   Store B

    C   Store C

    D   Store A and Store C

51. In a circle of any size, what ratio does pi (π) represent?

    A   the ratio of the radius to the diameter

    B   the ratio of the circumference to the diameter

    C   the ratio of the circumference to the radius

    D   the ratio of the circumference to the area

52. The Gleason family has a monthly budget of $4,500. Mr. Gleason has fulltime job and takes home $900 each week. Mrs. Gleason works part-time and brings home $9 for every hour she works. How many hours per month must Mrs. Gleason work to make sure that she and Mr. Gleason have met their monthly budget?

    A   10 h   C   50 h

    B   25 h   D   100 h

53. Jana has a bag of marbles. Without looking, she removes one marble from the bag, records the color, and replaces it. She repeats this process 50 times and records the results in the table.

Color	Frequency
Red	11
Blue	14
Green	9
Yellow	16

What is the probability that Jana will pick a blue marble on her fifty-first time?

A $\dfrac{9}{50}$ C $\dfrac{7}{25}$

B $\dfrac{11}{50}$ D $\dfrac{8}{25}$

54. Mills Middle School has 250 students. A random sample of 25 students were asked how many TVs they have at home. The results are shown in the dot plot below.

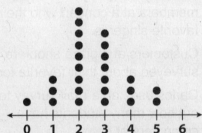

Which of the following is a qualitative statement that is reasonable based on the data?

    A   The fewest number of TVs at home is 1.

    B   Most students have 2 or fewer TVs at home.

    C   Most students have 3 or more TVs at home.

    D   The mean number of TVs students have at home is 2.

End-of-Year Test

55. Alim buys 2 T-shirts for $9.50 each, a 3-pack of socks for $7.95, and a pair of shoes for $49.95. The sales tax is 6%. To the nearest cent, what is the total cost of Alim's purchases?

_____

56. The probability of spinning an even number is 40%. What is the probability of **not** spinning an even number, written as a decimal?

_____

57. Tanya took a random survey of 20 sixth graders and 20 eighth graders. She asked how many hours a week each played video games. Her data is shown in the two dot plots below.

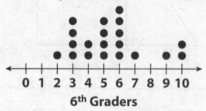

6th Graders

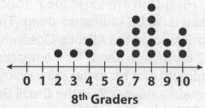

8th Graders

To the nearest tenth, what is the difference between the mean number of hours that 6th graders play video games and the mean number of hours that 8th graders play video games?

_____

58. A hockey player scores a goal on 35% of her attempts. Out of her next 20 attempts, how many times can you expect the player to score a goal?

_____

59. To the nearest tenth, what is the volume in cubic inches of the triangular prism below?

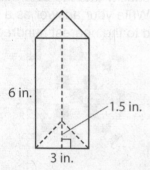

60. Bea's uncle said that if you subtract 15 from 3 times his age, you would get 60. Bea wrote this equation: $3x - 15 = 60$. How old is Bea's uncle?

_____

61. To the nearest hundredth, what is the area in square inches of the figure below? Use 3.14 for π.

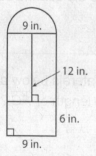

62. Jenna has $50 to spend at a local crafts fair. The entrance price for the fair is $10. At a pottery stand, Jenna finds some cups that she likes that are $4.50 each. What is the maximum number of cups that Jenna can buy?

_____

End-of-Year Test

63. A 7 ft-by-7 ft rug is shown below. A coin is tossed onto the rug randomly. What is the probability that the coin will land on black? Write your answer as a decimal rounded to the nearest hundredth.

_____

64. On a road map, the distance from New York City to Albany is 3 inches. The map scale is 1 in.:50 mi. How many miles is the actual distance between the two cities?

_____

65. Joanne's total score for a round of darts was −42. She had thrown 6 darts and scored the same on each throw. How many points did Joanne score on each throw?

_____

66. The quadrilaterals below are similar. What is the length of $\overline{FG}$?

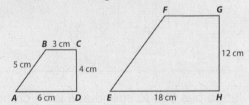

_____

67. According to the Royal Canadian Mint Act, a 50-cent Canadian coin must have a diameter of 27.13 millimeters. To the nearest hundredth, what is the circumference of this coin in millimeters?

_____

68. LaToya bought a new sofa for $2,900. She is entitled to an 11% rebate. How many dollars will the sofa cost after the rebate?

_____

69. In 5 years, twice a puppy's current age will be equal to or greater than 15. What is the least integer that satisfies the inequality $2x + 5 \geq 15$?

_____

70. To the nearest square meter, what is the area of the figure below?

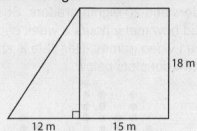

_____

71. The Philippine Trench in the Pacific Ocean is 10.05 kilometers deep. The Brazil Basin in the Atlantic Ocean is 6.12 kilometers deep. To the nearest hundredth of a kilometer, how many kilometers deeper than the Brazil Basin is the Philippine Trench?

_____

72. On a scale drawing, the image of an alligator is 7 inches long. The scale factor is $\frac{1}{25}$. What is the actual length of the alligator in inches?

_____

End-of-Year Test

73. Nauru and Gibraltar are the two smallest countries in the world. The area of Nauru is about 3.28 times the area of Gibraltar. The area of Gibraltar is 2.5 square miles. To the nearest tenth, what is the area of Nauru in square miles?

_____

74. There are 3,280.84 feet in a kilometer. There are 5,280 feet in a mile. To the nearest hundredth, how many kilometers are in a mile?

_____

75. A building has 9 floors. Each floor has 3 apartments. Omar made the spinners as a probability model for randomly choosing one apartment. Omar spins both the spinners below. What is the probability that the chosen apartment will be blue and above the 5th floor? Write your answer as a decimal rounded to the nearest hundredth.

_____

76. Each hour, the temperature dropped by $3\frac{1}{2}$ degrees. What was the change in temperature in $2\frac{1}{2}$ hours?

_____

77. One triangle has side lengths of 5 inches, 12 inches, and 13 inches. The side lengths of a second triangle are 15 inches, 36 inches, and 39 inches. What is the constant of proportionality between the two triangles?

_____

78. A supermarket is having a sale on canned foods. The sale includes 12 cans of soup for $10.65. What is the unit price per can of soup to the nearest cent?

_____

79. Beth says the graph below shows today's temperatures in degrees Celsius. What is the greatest temperature that is a solution to the inequality shown below?

```
◄——+——+——+——+——●——+——+——►
  -20  -10    0   10   20
```

_____

80. A larger circle contains white, striped, and black squares in the same ratio as those shown in the circle below. The larger circle contains 126 squares. How many of the squares are white? Write and solve a proportion to solve the problem.

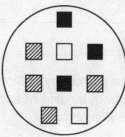

_____

81. A rectangular prism is 10 inches long, 6 inches wide, and 4 inches high. What is the surface area of this prism in square inches?

_____

82. What is the value of the expression below?

$$-3\left(-\frac{1}{6}\right)(-2)(2) \div \left(-\frac{1}{4}\right)$$

_____

End-of-Year Test

83. Four students put their game scores on the number line below. Which pair of students have a combined score of 0?

_____

84. Malorie wants to leave a 15% tip for the server at a restaurant. Which expression does **not** show how she can determine how much to leave if t is the total bill?

$0.15t$ $\qquad$ $t \div 0.15$ $\qquad$ $0.1t + 0.05t$

_____

85. Sam slices a rectangular prism with a plane parallel to the base. Describe the relationship between the two-dimensional shape (the cross section) that is sliced and the base of the prism.

_____

_____

86. What is the probability of flipping two coins and both landing heads? Give your answer as a decimal.

_____

87. You have three straws that are all the same length. Draw a picture of the triangle you can form with those straws. Tell what kind of triangle you drew.

_____

88. At a school carnival you pick a ball from two different containers. Each container has balls marked *A*, *B*, and *C*. Make a sample space that shows all the possible outcomes. Tell how many possible outcomes there are.

_____

89. A company knows that 30% of their customers who come to the store will check out the merchandise and then order it on-line because it is cheaper. The company wants to know the probability that it will take at least 3 customers to find one who shops on-line. How could the company find out this information?

_____

_____

90. Three students simplified the expression:
$2x - 3(y - 2x) + (-5)(-2y)$.

Their answers are below.

Amber: $-4x + 7y$

Butch: $4x + 7y$

Carl: $8x + 7y$

Tell who is correct. Explain the error the other students made.

_____

_____

Answer Key

Placement Test

1. B
2. D
3. D
4. D
5. C
6. A
7. D
8. B
9. A
10. B
11. C
12. B
13. B
14. D
15. C
16. D
17. B
18. A
19. C
20. C
21. A
22. B
23. D
24. C
25. B
26. D
27. D
28. A
29. C
30. A
31. C
32. A
33. C
34. B
35. C
36. A
37. C
38. C
39. C
40. C

Answer Key

Beginning-of-Year Diagnostic Test

1. **A** Correct

   $-7 + (-5) = -12°F$

   Students may use a number line, counting down from +5 to -7.

   TEST PREP DOCTOR: Students who answered **B** counted down from 0 instead of from +5. Students who answered **C** counted up from 0 to +5 rather than counting down from +5 to -7. Students who answered **D** counted up from -7 to +5 instead of counting down from +5 to -7.

2. **D** Correct

   The product of two negative integers is a positive integer.

   $(-12)(-5) = 60$

   TEST PREP DOCTOR: Students who answered **A** did not follow the product rules for signed integers: A negative times a negative results in a positive product. Students who answered **B** multiplied -12 by -4, not -5, and they failed to follow the product rule for signed number. Students who answered **C** multiplied -12 by -4, not -5.

3. **B** Correct

   Test values in the table to find that there is a 1 to 15 relationship between gallons and miles. So, there is a proportional relationship between miles and gallons.

   TEST PREP DOCTOR: Students who answered **A** may have been unable to spot a pattern in the table. Students who answered **C** reversed the proportion of gallons to miles. Students who answered **D** may have made a calculation error.

4. **A** Correct

   $\frac{4}{20} = \frac{2}{10} = 0.2$

   TEST PREP DOCTOR: Students who answered **B** may have made a calculation error. Students who answered **C** or **D** need to review how to convert a fraction to a decimal equivalent.

5. **B** Correct

   The constant of proportionality is the constant value k of the ratio of two proportional quantities x and y, where $y = kx$, or $k = \frac{y}{x}$. If x is the number of jars of honey and y is the total price, then $k = \frac{\text{total price}}{\text{number of jars}} = 4$.

   TEST PREP DOCTOR: Students who answered **A**, **C**, or **D** may have made a calculation error or need to review the concept of constant of proportionality.

6. **B** Correct

   $67 \div 7 \approx 9.57$

   Therefore, the number of complete bracelets Andrella can make is 9.

   TEST PREP DOCTOR: Students who answered **A** may have mistaken the divisor for the solution. Students who answered **C** rounded up. Andrella cannot make 10 bracelets since they would require 70 inches. Students who answered **D** may have made a calculation error.

7. **B** Correct

   $\frac{2000}{100} \times \frac{1}{10} = \frac{2000}{1000} = 2;$

   $60 + 2 = 62°F$

   TEST PREP DOCTOR: Students who answered **A** subtracted 2 instead of adding 2. Students who answered **C** made a calculation error, adding 12 instead of 2. Students who answered **D** may have divided 2,000 by 100 in the last step rather than 1,000, thereby adding 20 instead of adding 2.

8. **D** Correct

The unit rate that Tamara walked is the number of miles she walked per hour, so divide $\frac{3}{4}$ by $\frac{1}{2}$ to find the unit rate.

$$\frac{\frac{3}{4}}{\frac{1}{2}} = \frac{3}{4} \times \frac{2}{1} = \frac{6}{4} = \frac{3}{2} = 1\frac{1}{2}$$

So, the unit rate is $1\frac{1}{2}$ mi/h.

TEST PREP DOCTOR: Students who answered **A** or **C** may have made a conceptual error and need to review the concept of unit rate. Students who answered **B** divided the number of hours by the number of miles Tamara walked.

9. **A** Correct

$$\frac{1}{2}(2a + b) - (4a + b)$$

$$= \frac{1}{2}(2a) + \frac{1}{2}(b) - 4a - b$$

$$= a + \frac{1}{2}b - 4a - b$$

$$= -3a - \frac{1}{2}b$$

TEST PREP DOCTOR: Students who answered **B** forgot to multiply each coefficient by the respective second term. Students who answered **C** made a sign error in multiplying the second term. Students who answered **D** made a computation error.

10. **C** Correct

$$\frac{4}{6.40} = \frac{9}{x}$$

$$4x = 57.6$$

$$\frac{4x}{4} = \frac{57.6}{4}$$

$$x = 14.4 = \$14.40$$

TEST PREP DOCTOR: Students who answered **A** may have made a computational error. Students who answered **B** found the price of 8 muffins, not 9 muffins. Students who answered **D** moved the decimal point one extra place to the right.

11. **D** Correct

Since the scale factor is $\frac{1}{4}$ and the dimensions are given for the reduced rectangle, the student must multiply by 4 to find the full size: $12 \times 4 = 48$ in. and $16 \times 4 = 64$ in.

TEST PREP DOCTOR: Students who answered **A** applied the scale factor $\frac{1}{4}$ to the reduced triangle dimensions: $12 \times \frac{1}{4} = 3$ and $16 \times \frac{1}{4} = 4$. Students who answered **B** added 4 to each of the dimensions. Students who answered **C** multiplied the reduced dimensions by 3 instead of 4.

12. **A** Correct

$$-0.12 = -\frac{12}{100} \div \frac{4}{4} = -\frac{3}{25}$$

TEST PREP DOCTOR: Students who answered **B** converted -0.14 instead of -0.12. Students who answered **C** converted -0.12 incorrectly by dividing the numerator by 3 and the denominator by 4. Students who answered **D** did not simplify the numerator correctly.

13. **C** Correct

$$\frac{17.95}{2} = 8.975$$

$$5(8.975) = 44.875 \approx \$45$$

TEST PREP DOCTOR: Students who answered **A** rounded down to 17 and then doubled the dollars only. Students who answered **B** doubled the price and rounded up, but this product represents only 4 pounds of coffee, not 5. Students who answered **D** misplaced the decimal point in the original calculation and did not complete the second step of the problem.

14. **D** Correct

$$\frac{1}{25} = \frac{5.25}{x} = 131.25$$

To the nearest mile, that is 131 miles.

TEST PREP DOCTOR: Students who answered **A** may have made a calculation error, using 2.5 as a factor rather than 25. Students who answered **B** may have made a calculation error by adding 25 + 5.25. Students who answered **C** may have made a calculation error by multiplying 25 by 5, rounding down 5.25 to 5.

15. **C** Correct

$$12.39 - 10.50 = 1.89;$$

$$\frac{1.89}{10.50} = 0.18 = 18\%$$

TEST PREP DOCTOR: Students who answered **A** moved the decimal point one place to the right instead of 2 places. Students who answered **B** may have divided by her current wage instead of her initial wage. Students who answered **D** may have converted the difference in the first step of the problem into a percent.

16. **D** Correct

To solve the problem you must multiply the three measures.

$$11 \times 4 \times 4 = 176 \text{ cm}^3$$

TEST PREP DOCTOR: Students who answered **A** may have made a calculation error, adding the three measures: 4 + 4 + 11 = 19. Students who answered **B** may have made a calculation error, multiplying only two measures 11 × 4 = 44. Students who answered **C** may have made a calculation error, multiplying 11 × 4 × 2 = 88.

17. **C** Correct

$$\frac{4}{20} = 0.20 = 20\%$$

TEST PREP DOCTOR: Students who answered **A** may have made a computation error, placing the decimal two extra places to the left. Students who answered **B** may have placed the decimal point one extra place to the left. Students who answered **D** moved the decimal an extra place to the right.

18. **C** Correct

$$\frac{36\pi}{2\pi} = 18 \text{ in.}$$

TEST PREP DOCTOR: Students who answered **A** may have divided by 4π instead of 2π. Students who answered **B** may have divided by 3π instead of 2π. Students who answered **D** may have mistaken the diameter for the radius.

19. **A** Correct

The y-intercept is −2 and the slope is 1; therefore, the equation is $y = x − 2$, or $y + 2 = x$.

TEST PREP DOCTOR: Students who answered **B** misread the y-intercept as −1. Students who answered **C** misread the y-intercept as +1. Students who answered **D** misread the y-intercept as 2.

20. **C** Correct

Area of base: $10 \times 10 = 100 \text{ in}^2$

Area of one side: $\dfrac{10 \cdot 15}{2} = \dfrac{150}{2} = 75 \text{ in}^2$

SA (pyramid) = 100 + 4(75)
= 100 + 300 = 400 in^2

TEST PREP DOCTOR: Students who answered **A** added the area of the base and only one side. Students who answered **B** doubled the area of the base. Students who answered **D** incorrectly calculated the area of one side as 150 square inches, forgetting to divide by 2.

21. A Correct

$$\frac{2}{6} \cdot \frac{1}{2} = \frac{2}{12} = \frac{1}{6}$$

TEST PREP DOCTOR: Students who answered **B** forgot to multiply by $\frac{1}{2}$. Students who answered **C** added the numerators and then added the denominators. Students who answered **D** forgot to multiply by $\frac{1}{3}$.

22. C Correct

$$\frac{5.5}{220} = \frac{4}{x}$$

$$5.5x = 880$$

$$x = 160 \text{ mi}$$

TEST PREP DOCTOR: Students who answered **A** divided by 10 instead of 5.5. Students who answered **B** divided by 6 instead of 5.5 Students who answered **D** divided by 5 instead of 5.5.

23. B Correct

TEST PREP DOCTOR: Choice **A** is not random; the survey respondents are biased toward a particular sport. Choice **C** is not random; the selection of survey respondents is sequential. Choice **D** is incorrect because the survey respondents are not representative of all students.

24. B Correct

$$\frac{4}{14} = \frac{2}{x}$$

$$4x = 28$$

$$x = 7 \text{ in.}$$

TEST PREP DOCTOR: Students who answered **A** divided 14 by 4 instead of dividing by 2. Students who answered **C** may have made an error in computation, mistaking $14 \div 2$ as $16 \div 2$. Students who answered **D** multiplied by 2 instead of dividing by 2.

25. B Correct

$$\frac{9}{30} = \frac{3}{10} = 0.30 = 30\%, \text{ percent of red}$$

TEST PREP DOCTOR: Students who answered **A** calculated the percent of white marbles incorrectly; about 23% of the marbles are white. Students who answered **C** calculated the percent of blue marbles incorrectly; about 27% of the marbles are blue. Students who answered **D** calculated the percent of yellow marbles incorrectly; about 20% of the marbles are yellow.

26. C Correct

$$y = 2x + 6$$

$$y = 2(2) + 6$$

$$y = 10$$

TEST PREP DOCTOR: Students should determine if the x values in the table yield the y values shown. As shown above, if $x = 2$, then $y = 10$. Only table **C** shows these values. According to table **A**, when $x = 2$, then $y = 8$. According to table **B**, when $x = 2$, then $y = 8$. According to table **D**, when $x = 2$, then $y = 16$.

27. B Correct

$$15\frac{3}{8} = 15.375$$

TEST PREP DOCTOR: Students who answered **A** found the decimal equivalent of $15\frac{1}{8}$. Students who answered **C** or **D** may have made a computation error.

28. D Correct

$$P(\text{red}) = \frac{2}{8}$$

$$P(\text{green}) = \frac{3}{8}$$

$$\frac{2}{8} + \frac{3}{8} = \frac{5}{8}$$

TEST PREP DOCTOR: Students who answered **A** only calculated the probability of landing on red. Students who answered **B** only calculated the probability of landing on green. Students who answered **C** probably made a calculation error.

29. **D** Correct

TEST PREP DOCTOR: Choice **A** is incorrect because set A has a mode of 50, whereas set B has a mode of 30. Choice **B** is incorrect because set A has 11 items, whereas set B has 12 items. Choice **C** is incorrect because set B is more symmetric than set A.

30. **D** Correct

$3 \times 3 \times 2 = 18$ outfits

TEST PREP DOCTOR: Students who answered **A** multiplied 3 by 2 instead of multiplying 3 by 3 by 2. Students who answered **B** added the factors instead of multiplying them. Students who answered **C** multiplied 3 by 3 instead of multiplying 3 by 3 by 2.

31. **B** Correct

$6 \times 8 = 48$ cm^2;

$2(5 \times 8) = 80$ cm^2;

$\frac{1}{2}(6)(4)(2) = 24$ cm^2;

$48 + 80 + 24 = 152$ cm^2

TEST PREP DOCTOR: Students who answered **A** failed to add the area of the triangles. Students who answered **C** calculated the area of the triangles incorrectly, failing to divide by 2. Students who answered **D** multiplied the correct factors by an additional factor of 2.

32. **C** Correct

$\frac{28}{40} = 0.70$;

$470 \times 0.70 = 329$ students

TEST PREP DOCTOR: Students who answered **A** multiplied 470 by 0.28 and then rounded up. Students who answered **B** multiplied 470 by

0.40. Students who answered **D** multiplied 470 by 0.72 and rounded down.

33. **A** Correct

$$-5x - 10 < 20$$
$$-5x - 10 + 10 < 20 + 10$$
$$-5x < 30$$
$$\frac{-5x}{-5} < \frac{30}{-5}$$
$$x > -6$$

TEST PREP DOCTOR: Students who answered **B** subtracted 10 from 20 on the right side of the inequality instead of adding 10. Students who answered **C** failed to reverse the inequality sign. Students who answered **D** subtracted 10 from 20 on the right side of the equation and also failed to reverse the inequality sign.

34. **D** Correct

Let x represent the number of hours of dog walking and then add $15.

$y = 5x + 15$

TEST PREP DOCTOR: Students who answered **A** multiplied x by 15 instead of 5 and subtracted the constant 5 instead of adding it. Students who answer **B** multiplied the variable by 15 instead of 5 and added the wrong constant. Student who answered **C** subtracted the constant 15 instead of adding it.

35. **C** Correct

Area of rectangle: $l \times w = 6 \times 4 = 24$ in^2;

Areas of triangle: $\frac{1}{2} bh = \frac{1}{2}(6 \times 3) = \frac{18}{2} = 9$ in^2;

Area of semicircle: $\pi r^2 \div 2 = (3.14)(2^2) \div 2 = (3.14)(4) \div 2 = 12.56 \div 2 = 6.28$ in^2;

$24 + 9 + 6.28 \approx 39.3$ in^2

TEST PREP DOCTOR: Students who answered **A** did not add the area of the triangle. Students who answered **B** did not add the area of the semicircle. Students who answered **D** did not calculate the area of the triangle correctly, failing to divide by 2.

36. C Correct

$\angle DGE$ and $\angle BGD$ are supplementary angles and $\angle DGE = 90°$, so $180° - 90° = 90°$.

TEST PREP DOCTOR: Students who answered **A** may have calculated the measure of $\angle BGC$. Students who answered **B** may have calculated the measure of $\angle CGD$. Students who answered **D** subtracted the measure of $\angle CGD$ from $\angle BGE$: $180° - 50° = 130°$.

37. C Correct

$\$5,000 \times 0.15 = \$750$

TEST PREP DOCTOR: Students who answered **A** multiplied 5,000 by 0.05. Students who answered **B** multiplied 5,000 by 0.10. Students who answered **D** multiplied 5,000 by 0.22.

38. D Correct

$30 \times 16 \times 14 = 6,720 \text{ in}^3$

TEST PREP DOCTOR: Students who answered **A** multiplied only two factors: 14 by 16. Students who answered **B** multiplied only two factors: 30 by 14. Students who answered **C** multiplied only two factors: 30 by 16.

39. C Correct

$A = \pi r^2$

$A = (3.14)(7^2)$

$A = (3.14)(49) = 153.86 \text{ in}^2$

TEST PREP DOCTOR: Students who answered **A** did not raise 7 to the power of 2. ($7^2 = 49$). Students who answered **B** multiplied 7 by 2 ($7 \times 2 = 14$) instead of raising 7 to the power of 2 ($7^2 = 49$). Students who

answered **D** raised 14 instead of 7 to the power of 2 ($14^2 = 196$).

40. B Correct

$800 \times 0.05 = 40$ people

TEST PREP DOCTOR: Students who answered **A** multiplied 400 by 2.5%, or 0.025. Students who answered **C** multiplied 800 by 10%, or 0.10. Students who answered **D** multiplied 800 by 15%, or 0.15.

41. B Correct

TEST PREP DOCTOR: Choice **A** is not random; the selection of survey respondents is sequential. Choice **C** is incorrect because the survey respondents are biased toward friends of the manager. Choice **D** is incorrect because the survey respondents are biased toward the best equestrian riders at the stable.

42. C Correct

$\dfrac{16}{40.64} = \dfrac{42}{x}$

$16x = 1706.68$

$x = 106.68 \text{ cm}$

TEST PREP DOCTOR: Students who answered **A** added $16 + 40.64$ instead of multiplying these factors. Students who answered **B** added $40.64 + 42$. Students who answered **D** multiplied 40.64 by 42.

43. C Correct

diameter of second circle is $6 \times 4 = 24$;

ratio of areas: $= \dfrac{9\pi}{144\pi} = \dfrac{1}{16}$

TEST PREP DOCTOR: Students who answered **A** or **B** wrote an incorrect ratio. Students who answered **D** used the diameter instead of the radius for the larger circle in the formula for area.

44. C Correct

The center line of the box indicates the median: 40.

TEST PREP DOCTOR: Students who answered **A** selected the least number of the data set. Students who answered **B** selected the median of the lower quartile instead of the median of the entire data set. Students who answered **D** selected the median of the upper quartile.

45. B Correct

The interquartile range is the absolute value of the difference between the values at the two ends of the box.

$|45 - 25| = 20$

TEST PREP DOCTOR: Students who answered **A** selected the least number of the data set. Students who answered **C** selected the median of the data set. Students who answered **D** selected the median of the upper quartile.

46. C Correct

$\angle FGE = 180 - 110 = 70$, so $5x + 6x + 70 = 180$. Solve for x:

$5x + 6x = 180 - 70$

$11x = 110$

$x = 10$

$\angle FEG = 5x$

$5x = 5(10) = 50$

TEST PREP DOCTOR: Students who answered **A** or **B** may have made a computation error. Students who answered **D** found the measure of $\angle FGE$.

47. A Correct

$5x = 50$ and $6x = 60$, so $5x + 6x = 110$.

TEST PREP DOCTOR: Students who answered **B, C,** or **D** may have made a computation error or need to review the concepts of triangle sums and supplementary and adjacent angles.

48. A Correct

Every x-value in the table results in the corresponding y-value.

TEST PREP DOCTOR: Students who answered **B** or **C** may have checked only the first x-value in the table. made a computation error. Students who answered **D** may have made a calculation error.

49. B Correct

$x - 2 \geq 3$

$x \geq 3 + 2$

$x \geq 5$

TEST PREP DOCTOR: Students who selected **A** misread the graph which represents $x \leq -5$ and reversed the inequality sign. Students who selected **C** subtracted 4 from 3 and reversed the inequality sign; the graph represents $x \leq -1$. Students who selected **D** subtracted 4 from 3; the graph represents $x \geq -1$.

50. D Correct

Store $A = 150 \times 0.15 = 22.50$; $150 - 22.50 = \$127.50$

Store $B = 150 - 25 = \$125.00$

Store $C = 150 - 20 = \$130.00$

Store $D = \$120.00$

TEST PREP DOCTOR: Students who answered **A, B,** or **C** made an error in calculation or comparison.

51. B Correct

$d = 12; r = 6$

TEST PREP DOCTOR: Students who answered **A** divided the diameter by 4 instead of 2. Students who answered **C** failed to divide 12 by 2. Students who answered **D** multiplied 12 by 2.

52. C Correct

$5,500 - 4,000 = 1,500$;

$1,500 \div 16 = 93.75$

TEST PREP DOCTOR: Students who answered **A** divided 1,500 by 40 instead of dividing 1,500 by 16. Students who answered **B** divided 1,500 by 20. Students who answered **D** divided 1,500 by 12.

53. C Correct

35 of the 40 tiles are not yellow.

$$\frac{35}{40} = \frac{7}{8}$$

TEST PREP DOCTOR: Students who answered **A** found the probability of choosing a yellow tile. Students who answered **B** probably multiplied 5 by 2 and wrote it over 40. Students who answered **D** incorrectly found $\frac{36}{40}$.

54. B Correct

22 out of 30 students have 2 or fewer cars at home.

TEST PREP DOCTOR: Students who answered **A** did not notice that 4 students had 0 cards at home. Students who answered **C** failed to calculate that only 8 out 31 students have 3 or more cars at home. Students who answered **D** mistook the middle number on the *x*-axis for the median.

55. C Correct

Ties: 19.95 × 3 = $59.85

Subtotal: 59.85 + 23.50 + 124.95 = $208.30

Tax: 208.30 × 0.05 = $10.415

Total: 208.30 + 10.415 = 218.715 ≈ $218.72

TEST PREP DOCTOR: Students who answered **A** calculated the total with 1 tie, not 3 ties. Students who answered **B** calculated the total with 2 ties, not 3 ties. Students who answered **D** calculated the total with 2 pairs of boots and 2 ties.

56. B Correct

To find the probability of not spinning an odd number, subtract the probability of spinning an odd number from 100%.

100% − 62% = 38%

= 0.38

TEST PREP DOCTOR: Students who answered **A** and **C** subtracted incorrectly. Students who answered **D** selected the percent given in the problem as the answer.

57. A Correct

The mode is the value in each set with the most data points. The mode for sixth graders is 5 hours. The mode for eighth graders is 8 hours.

8 − 5 = 3 h

TEST PREP DOCTOR: Students who answered **B** selected 5, the mode for 6th graders. Students who answered **C** selected 8, the mode for eighth graders Students who answered **D** found the sum of the modes instead of the difference.

58. B Correct

Multiply the specified number of future at bats by the experimental probability of getting a hit on any at bat, 20%.

15 × 0.20 = 3 hits.

TEST PREP DOCTOR: Students who answered **A** may have miscalculated 20% of 15 as 2.

Students who answered **C** found $\frac{1}{3}$ or 33.33% of 15. Students who answered **D** found 80% of 15.

59. A Correct

$$V(\text{triangular prism}) = \frac{1}{2}lwh$$

Substitute the given dimensions into the formula.

$$V = \frac{1}{2}(4)(5)(10)$$

$$= \frac{200}{2}$$

$$= 100 \text{ cm}^3$$

TEST PREP DOCTOR: Students who answered **B** or **C** made a multiplication error. Students who selected **D** forgot to divide the product of the three dimensions by 2.

60. D Correct

$$5x - 35 = 40$$
$$5x - 35 + 35 = 40 + 35$$
$$5x = 75$$
$$x = 15$$

TEST PREP DOCTOR: Students who answered **A** subtracted 40 from 35 and then divided both sides by 5. $(35 - 40 = -5; -5 \div 5 = -1)$ Students who answered **B** subtracted 35 from the right side of the equation and then divided both sides by 5. Students who selected **C** added $(-40) + (-35) = -75$, and then divided both sides by 5.

61. A Correct

A(rectangle) $= 8 \times 4 = 32$ in^2

A(semicircle) $= (3.14)(4^2) \div 2$
$$= (3.14)(16) \div 2$$
$$= 25.12 \text{ in}^2$$

A(figure) $= 32 + 25.12 = 57.12$ in^2

TEST PREP DOCTOR: Students who answered **B** calculated the area of the rectangle as $2l \times 2w = 16 \times 8 = 128$. Students who answered **C** calculated the area of the circular portion incorrectly as πd^2: $3.14 \times 64 = 200.96$. Students who answered **D** added the calculations shown above for **B** and **C**.

62. B Correct

After paying the entrance fee, Mike has $75 - 20 = \$55$.

Divide $55 by the price per car of $7.50.

$$\frac{55}{7.50} = 7.3333...$$

Mike cannot buy a fraction of a car, so round down to the nearest whole number. Mike can buy 7 cars.

TEST PREP DOCTOR: Students who answered **A** subtracted $75 - 25 = 50$ and then divided 50 by 7.5. Students who answered **C** did the calculation correctly but then rounded

up instead of rounding down. Students who answered **D** may have incorrectly calculated $75 \div 7.5$.

63. C Correct

The rug is divided into 49 equal squares. An area equal to 36 of the squares is white.

$$\frac{36}{49} = 0.73469$$

The probability of landing on a white section is 73.47%.

TEST PREP DOCTOR: Students who answered **A** set up the proportion incorrectly as $\frac{13}{49}$. Students who answered **B** set up the proportion incorrectly as $\frac{13}{36}$. Students who answered **D** set up the proportion incorrectly as $\frac{36}{13}$.

64. C Correct

$$\frac{1 \text{ in.}}{25 \text{ mi}} = \frac{2 \text{ in.}}{\text{actual distance}}$$

actual distance $= 2\left(\frac{25}{1}\right) = 50$

So, the actual distance is 50 miles.

TEST PREP DOCTOR: Students who answered **A** set up the proportion incorrectly. Students who answered **B** found the actual distance of 1 inch. Students who answered **D** may have made a computation error.

65. A Correct

$$3 + x = -15$$
$$x = -12$$
$$\frac{-12}{6} = -2$$

So, the change in temperature each hour was $-2°$.

TEST PREP DOCTOR: Students who answered **B** may have made a computation error. Students who answered **C** or **D** misinterpreted the question and made computation errors.

66. B Correct

Choose corresponding dimensions of the two figures, and set up a proportion to determine the scale factor.

$$\frac{AD}{EH} = \frac{6}{18} = \frac{1}{3}$$

The unknown length *EF* in the larger figure corresponds to *AB* in the smaller figure, which has a length of 5 cm.

Set up another proportion comparing the scale factor to the lengths of *AB* and *EF*.

$$\frac{1}{3} = \frac{5}{EF}$$

$$EF = 15$$

TEST PREP DOCTOR: Students who answered **A** set up the ratio incorrectly, using non-corresponding sides of the two figures. Students who answered **C** set up the ratio incorrectly, using non-corresponding sides of the two figures, and then misplaced the decimal point. Students who answered **D** set up the ratio incorrectly, using non-corresponding sides of the two figures, and then rounded up.

67. A Correct

Substitute the given values into the formula for he circumference of a circle.

$$C = \pi d$$

$$C = (3.14)(28)$$

$$C = 87.92 \text{ mm}$$

TEST PREP DOCTOR: Students who answered **B** may have used the incorrect formula $C = 2\pi d$. Students who answered **C** may have used the incorrect formula $C = \pi r^2$. Students who answered **D** may have used the incorrect formula $C = \pi d^2$.

68. C Correct

To find the amount of the rebate, multiply the price of the truck by the percent rebate.

$$36{,}000 \times 0.08 = \$2{,}880$$

Subtract this rebate amount from the truck price.

$$36{,}000 - 2{,}880 = \$33{,}120$$

TEST PREP DOCTOR: Students who answered **A** may have calculated the rebate and incorrectly multiplied by 10. Students who answered **B** incorrectly calculated the rebate as 18%. Students who answered **D** likely guessed.

69. D Correct

$5 times the number of hours plus the $10 bike rental fee must be less than or equal to $25, so you could use the inequality $5x + 10 \leq 25$ to find *x*, the number of hours Sofia could rent a bike.

TEST PREP DOCTOR: Students who answered **A** or **C** transposed the rental fee and per-hour rental rate and chose the wrong inequality sign. **B** chose the wrong inequality sign.

70. C Correct

$$A(\text{rectangle}) = 5 \times 8 = 40 \text{ m}^2$$

$$A(\text{triangle}) = \frac{1}{2}bh$$

$$= \frac{1}{2}(4)(8) = 16 \text{ m}^2$$

$$A(\text{figure}) = 40 + 16 = 56 \text{ m}^2$$

TEST PREP DOCTOR: Students who answered **A** may have found only the area of the triangle and forgotten to multiply by $\frac{1}{2}$. Students who answered **B** failed to include the area of the triangular part of the figure. Students who answered **D** failed to multiply by $\frac{1}{2}$ when finding the area of the triangular region.

71. B Correct

To find the difference in the two elevations, subtract the original elevation of the bird from the elevation of the Dead Sea.

$-1{,}360 - (-422) = -938$ ft

TEST PREP DOCTOR: Students who answered **A** added both elevations:

$(-1{,}360) + (-422) = -1{,}782$. Students who answered **C** ignored the negative signs in the elevations and subtracted $1360 - 422 = 938$. Students who answered **D** may have added the two elevations without their negative signs: $1{,}360 + 422 = 1{,}782$.

72. C Correct

Set up a proportion that relates the scale factor to the length of the image of the alligator and the actual length of the alligator.

$$\frac{1}{25} = \frac{\text{image length}}{\text{actual length}}$$

$$\frac{1}{25} = \frac{7}{x}$$

Cross multiply.

$1x = 7 \times 25$

$x = 175$ in.

TEST PREP DOCTOR: Students who answered **A** may have multiplied the image length by the scale factor, then misplaced the decimal point:

$7 \times \frac{1}{25} = \frac{7}{25} = 0.28 \neq 28$. Students who answered **B** may have multiplied the reciprocal of the image length by the reciprocal of the scale factor, then placed the decimal point incorrectly:

$\frac{1}{7} \times 25 = \frac{25}{7} = 3.57 \neq 35.7$. Students who answered **D** set up the problem incorrectly and used the wrong decimal, representing $\frac{1}{25}$ as 0.025.

73. C Correct

Since the area of Bermuda is 1.8 times the area of Norfolk Island, multiply the area of Norfolk Island by 1.8.

$36 \times 1.8 = 64.8$ km^2

TEST PREP DOCTOR: Students who answered **A** multiplied by $\frac{1}{8}$ instead of 1.8. Students who answered **B** multiplied by 0.18 instead of 1.8. Students who answered **D** multiplied by 18 instead of 1.8.

74. B Correct

$$\frac{21{,}280.08}{12} = 1{,}773.34$$

TEST PREP DOCTOR: Students who answered **A** made an error in placing the decimal. Students who answered **C** or **D** may have made a computation error.

75. C Correct

To find the probability of a compound event, multiply the probabilities of the individual events.

On the color spinner, 2 of 6 equal sections are red.

$$P(\text{red}) = \frac{2}{6} = \frac{1}{3}$$

On the number spinner, 4 of the 9 sections (1, 3, and 4) have a value less than 5.

$$P(< 5) = \frac{4}{9}$$

$$P(\text{red and} < 5) = \frac{1}{3} \cdot \frac{4}{9} = \frac{4}{27}$$

TEST PREP DOCTOR: Students who answered **A** incorrectly represented the $P(\text{red})$ as $\frac{3}{32}$ and the $P(< 5)$ as $\frac{1}{6}$. Students who answered **B** incorrectly represented the $P(\text{red})$ as $\frac{1}{4}$, perhaps basing their calculation on the spinner having 8, rather than 6, sectors. Students who answered **D** incorrectly represented the $P(< 5)$ as $\frac{5}{9}$, including 1, 2, 3, 4, and 5 as desired outcomes, although 5 is not less than 5.

76. **B** Correct

Multiply the change in temperature per hour by the number of hours.

$$1\frac{1}{2} \times 1\frac{1}{2} = \frac{3}{2} \times \frac{3}{2} = \frac{9}{4} = 2\frac{1}{4}$$

TEST PREP DOCTOR: Students who answered **A** or **C** may have made a computation error. Students who answered **D** added the change in temperature per hour to the number of hours.

77. **B** Correct

To find the constant of proportionality, write a ratio that feature any pair of corresponding side lengths from the second and first triangle, then simplify.

$$\frac{8}{48} = \frac{1}{6}$$

TEST PREP DOCTOR: Students who answered **A** may have set up a ratio of non-corresponding side lengths $\left(\frac{8}{90}\right)$, and then made a calculation error:

$\frac{8}{90} = \frac{4}{44} = \frac{1}{11}$. Students who answered **C** set up a ratio between the second and first triangles:

$\frac{48}{8} = 6$. Students who answered **D** may have set up a ratio of non-corresponding side lengths $\left(\frac{90}{8}\right)$, and then made a calculation error:
$\frac{90}{8} = \frac{44}{4} = 11$.

78. **B** Correct

To find the price per can, divide the total price by the number of cans of beans.

$$\frac{12.50}{10} = 1.25$$

TEST PREP DOCTOR: Students who answered **A** divided the number of cans by the total price. Students who answered **C** or **D** may have made a computation error.

79. **D** Correct

The graph shows that last year's temperatures were less than or equal to 10°. The only answer that is NOT less than or equal to 10° is 10.3°.

TEST PREP DOCTOR: Students who answered **A**, **B**, or **C** may have misinterpreted the graph and need to review the concept of inequalities.

80. **B** Correct

The small circle shown contains 9 squares, and the larger circle contains 162 squares, so there are $162 \div 9 = 18$ times as many squares in the larger circle. To find the number of black squares in the larger circle multiply the number of black squares in the small circle (3) by 18.

$3 \cdot 18 = 54$ gray squares.

TEST PREP DOCTOR: Students who answered **A** found the number of white squares. Students who answered **C** found the number of striped squares. Students who answered **D** found the number of black squares and added that to the number of white squares.

81. **B** Correct

Find the surface area of the prism.
$2(5 \times 2) + 2(5 \times 2) + 2(2 \times 2)$
$= 2(10) + 2(10) + 2(4)$
$= 20 + 20 + 8$
$= 48$

TEST PREP DOCTOR: Students who answered **A** found the volume of the prism. Students who answered **C** or **D** may have made a computation error.

82. **B** Correct

$$-3\left(\frac{1}{6}\right)(2) \div \frac{1}{4}$$

$$= -1 \div \frac{1}{4}$$

$$= -4$$

TEST PREP DOCTOR: Students who answered **A** forgot to multiply the 2 in the first term. Students who answered **C** or **D** may have made a computation error.

83. **B** Correct

Add the scores of students B and D.
$$-3 + 3 = 0$$

TEST PREP DOCTOR: Students who answered **A** found the combined score of students B and C. Students who answered **C** or **D** may have made a computation error.

84. **C** Correct

Ava should leave the price of the meal plus 20% times the price of the meal, or $m + 0.2m$.

TEST PREP DOCTOR: Students who answered **A** misrepresented the tip amount and did not include the meal price. Students who answered **B** chose the expression that represents only the tip. Students who answered **D** misrepresented the tip amount

85. **C** Correct

A rectangular prism sliced by a horizontal plane will have a cross-section shaped like a rectangle.

TEST PREP DOCTOR: Students who answered **A**, **B**, or **D** need to review the possible shapes of cross-sections that result from slicing three-dimensional figures.

86. **A** Correct

Multiply the probability of flipping a coin and landing tails by the probability of flipping another coin and landing tails.

$$\frac{1}{2} \times \frac{1}{2} = \frac{1}{4} = 0.25$$

TEST PREP DOCTOR: Students who answered **B**, **C**, or **D** need to review the concept of compound probability.

87. **C** Correct

The line segments cannot form a triangle because the sum of the two shorter sides must be greater than the length of the longest side.

TEST PREP DOCTOR: Students who answered **A**, **B**, or **D** need to review the conditions for possible triangles.

88. **B** Correct

There are 4 possible outcomes:
red ball, red ball
red ball, green ball
green ball, green ball
green ball, red ball

TEST PREP DOCTOR: Students who answered **A** did not consider enough possible outcomes. Students who answered **C** or **D** may have counted the same outcome more than once.

89. **D** Correct

The theoretical probability of a customer walking into Andy's deli and purchasing a sandwich is 6 in 10, or 0.6, so the prediction that is most likely true is 12 out of the next 20 customers will purchase a sandwich, which is the same theoretical probability as 0.6.

TEST PREP DOCTOR: Students who answered **A**, **B**, or **C** need to review the concept of theoretical probability.

90. A Correct

$$2x - 3(y - 2x)$$
$$= 2x - 3y + 6x$$
$$= 8x - 3y$$

TEST PREP DOCTOR: Students who answered **B** forgot to multiply -3 by $2x$. Students who answered **C** made a sign error when multiplying -3 by $2x$. Students who answered **D** made a computation error.

Answer Key
Module Quizzes

MODULE 1 Adding and Subtracting Integers

Module Quiz 1: B

1. B
2. B
3. B
4. A
5. A
6. D
7. D
8. A
9. A
10. D
11. B
12. C
13. $15
14. $400 - 50 + 20 - 150$
15. Answers will vary. Sample answer: $2 - 6 + 2$
16. 16 ft
17. y must be negative in order to have a negative sum.
18. -1
19. City C
20. $x < y$
21. No. If the absolute value of the first number is greater than the number being subtracted, the difference will be negative.
22. 3, -5, 8. Each number in the sequence is the difference of the previous two numbers.

Module Quiz 1: D

1. A
2. C
3. A
4. A
5. A

6. C
7. A
8. A
9. C
10. B
11. A
12. $60
13. $100 - 75$
14. $-2 + 4$
15. 101 ft
16. Answers will vary. Sample answer: Subtracting a negative number has the same effect as adding a positive number. Since 10 is positive, 10 plus a positive number will always be positive.
17. 5
18. -35
19. -1
20. 4°
21. 7
22. -9
23. -10, -12, -14. Subtract 2 to get each successive term.
24. -2, 0, -2. Add 2 then subtract 2.

MODULE 2 Multiplying and Dividing Integers

Module Quiz 2: B

1. A
2. D
3. B
4. D
5. B
6. B
7. B
8. C
9. B

10. $\dfrac{63 - (-21)}{12} = 7$; The temperature decreased by an average of 7° per hour, so the average change per hour is negative: −7°.

11. a. Sample answer: $(-4)(-3)(-6) = -72$
    b. Make one factor positive.

12. $4(-2) = -8$; 8 in. shorter

13. $5(-4) + 3 = -17$

14. $\dfrac{(-72) + 4 + (-12)}{10} = -8$

15. $6(-69) = -414$

16. $3(75) + (-55) + (-104) + (-85) + 3 = -16$ points

17. $\dfrac{-1,044}{6} = -174$; He lost an average of 174 points per game.

18. $8(-3) + 6 = -18$ in.

19. $12(-8) = -96$ in.

Module Quiz 2: D
1. C
2. B
3. A
4. C
5. B
6. A
7. C
8. B
9. B
10. −3°
11. Change one factor to positive or change all factors to positive.
12. −200 m
13. −108 points
14. −210 in.
15. −15
16. −12 in.
17. −25 ft
18. addition
19. −$8
20. −23
21. −56

MODULE 3 Rational Numbers

Module Quiz 3: B
1. A
2. D
3. B
4. A
5. A
6. A
7. D
8. B
9. D
10. A
11. $63
12. $-\dfrac{8}{15}$
13. −21.925
14. $145
15. $600
16. 700
17. $8.43
18. 9
19. $\dfrac{23}{40}$
20. $\dfrac{3}{5}$ lb
21. $\dfrac{3}{4}$ of the distance
22. $\dfrac{17}{36}$ of the box

Module Quiz 3: D
1. C
2. A
3. B
4. B
5. B
6. B
7. A
8. C
9. B
10. C
11. 120

12. $68

13. $\frac{37}{7}$

14. $145

15. 3.5 hr

16. $35

17. 1.36

18. 2.25 lb

19. 60 mph

20. 18 minutes

21. $1,250 loss

22. $82.50

23. $300

24. $-1\frac{1}{5}$

MODULE 4 Rates and Proportionality

Module Quiz 4: B

1. C

2. A

3. B

4. D

5. C

6. D

7. A

8. D

9. $\frac{1}{5}$; $\frac{3}{10}$

10. 21.6 mi

11. Divide 330 by $\frac{3}{4}$. This equals 330 times $\frac{4}{3}$, which equals 440. The result shows the number of pages per hour, or the unit rate.

12. $k = 6.4$; $y = 6.4x$

13. Answers will vary. Sample answer:

Number of Cookies	6	12	20
Cost ($)	15	30	50

14. Sample graph shown. Location of points will vary.

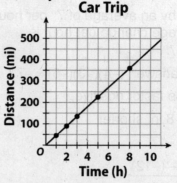

Car Trip

15. $y = 15x$

16. Answers will vary. Sample answer: $y = 30x$

Savings Account

17. 1.6 mi/h

Module Quiz 4: D

1. C

2. A

3. C

4. B

5. B

6. B

7. C

8. B

9. 40; 60

10. 4.8 mi

11. $\frac{10}{3}$; $1\frac{2}{3}$ mi/h

12. Each value of x is multiplied by 10 to get the value of y.

13. Answers will vary. Sample answer: 10 lbs cost $100

Number of Pounds	1	2	3
Cost ($)	$10	$20	$30

14. Sample graph shown. Location of points will vary. All points satisfy the equation $y = 2x$.

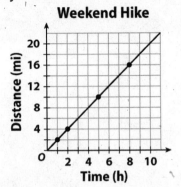

Weekend Hike

15. $75
16. Answers will vary; Sample answer: (1, 15), (2, 30)
17. 12.44 mi/h

MODULE 5 Proportions and Percent

Module Quiz 5: B

1. C
2. B
3. D
4. C
5. D
6. C
7. C
8. C
9. A
10. C
11. Sample answer: Find 2.7% of $55.80 and add the result to $55.80.
12. Sample answer: Multiply $55.80 by 1.027.
13. $133.75
14. 29.6% decrease
15. Riverview with an increase of 51%
16. $609.70
17. $197.40
18. $79.50
19. $8,360
20. $19.07
21. $k = 6.5$; $y = 6.5x$

Module Quiz 5: D

1. C
2. B
3. A
4. B
5. A
6. B
7. C
8. B
9. A
10. B
11. Sample answer: Find 2% of $57 and add it to $57.
12. Sample answer: Multiply 57 by 1.02.
13. $201.25
14. 10.7%
15. 51.1%
16. $3.90
17. $90
18. 8%
19. $150
20. $2.33
21. $y = 50x$

MODULE 6 Expressions and Equations

Module Quiz 6: B

1. D
2. C
3. C
4. A
5. A
6. C
7. C
8. A
9. A
10. B
11. C
12. $2.50x = 90$; 36 times
13. 6 games
14. 30 shirts

15. Sample answer: $\dfrac{m}{2} + 6$

16. three tenths of a number plus 5

17. 4 dimes = \$0.40; some nickels = \$0.05x;
    $0.4 + 0.05x = 2.25$

18. $x = 40$

19. He divided 6 by 3 instead of −3 in Step 3.

20. $2{,}500 + 0.08s = 5{,}400$

21. $50 - 12.25p$

22. $50 + 12.50x = 400$; $x = 28$

Module Quiz 6: D

1. B
2. A
3. C
4. A
5. B
6. A
7. A
8. A
9. C
10. B
11. $5.50x \le 108.50$; $x \le 19.73$; She can buy 19 shirts.
12. $x = -30$
13. 4
14. $5x + 200 = 450$; $x = 50$
15. 20 nickels
16. \$160
17. In Step 2 she subtracted 4 instead of adding 4.
18. \$40,000 + \$1,000x = \$60,000; $x = 20$
19. 200
20. $100 + 20x = 400$; $x = 15$
21. $2.75n = 80$; $n \approx 29.09$; He can ride the train 29 times.
22. $y = 12\left(\dfrac{6}{5}\right) = \dfrac{72}{5} = 14\dfrac{2}{5}$

MODULE 7 Inequalities

Module Quiz 7: B

1. D
2. D
3. C
4. A
5. C
6. C
7. B
8. C
9. B
10. A
11. C
12. $\dfrac{x}{6} \le 1$

    $6\left(\dfrac{x}{6}\right) \le 6(1)$

    $x \le 6$

13. $x + 8 \ge 5$

    $x + 8 - 8 \ge 5 - 8$

    $x \ge -3$

14.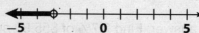

15. To solve first inequality you have to divide by a negative number, so you have to reverse the inequality symbol. To solve second inequality, you divide by a positive number so the inequality symbol stays the same.

16. $x < -3$

17. $x > -3$

18. He forgot to reverse the inequality symbol in Step 3.

19. $4{,}000 + 0.06s \ge 7{,}000$

20. $15x \le 75$

    $\dfrac{15x}{15} \le \dfrac{75}{15}$

    $x \le 5$; Betsy can pay for no more than 5 months of the service fee.

Module Quiz 7: D

1. C
2. A
3. C
4. A
5. A
6. A
7. A
8. A
9. C
10. C
11. $300 - 20x > 100$
12. $x > -15$
13. 5
14. Add 4 to both sides of the inequality to isolate the variable
15. $x - 4 \leq 3$
    $x - 4 + 4 \leq 3 + 4$
    $x \leq 7$
16.
17. In Step 2, he should have added 4 to each side of the inequality to undo the subtraction of 4. He subtracted 4 instead.
18. multiply; divide; negative; reverse; true
19. 200
20. The inequality with the $\leq$ sign would include 3 as part of the solution. The inequality with the $<$ sign would not include 3 as part of the solution.
21.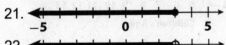
22.

MODULE 8 Modeling Geometric Figures

Module Quiz 8: B

1. A
2. B
3. D
4. D
5. B
6. B
7. B
8. C
9. A
10. B
11. 2,091 m²
12. Students' rectangles should be 3 units tall and 10 units wide.
13. a unique triangle
14. Students' triangles should have angles measuring 40°, 50° and 90° and an included side measuring 2 inches.
15. $37.63
16. circle
17. Yes, if a vertical plane intersected the cylinder, the cross section would be a rectangle.
18. 133°
19. supplementary angles
20. 26 bags

Module Quiz 8: D

1. B
2. C
3. C
4. C
5. B
6. B
7. B
8. C
9. A
10. B
11. 1 unit: 10 ft
12. 27,000 m²
13. unique
14. Students' triangles should have angles measuring 60°, 60° and 60° and three side lengths each measuring 2 inches.
15. $21
16. circle
17. Students' sketches should be a circle shape.

18. 150°

19. adjacent angles

20. 6 bags

MODULE 9 Circumference, Area, and Volume

Module Quiz 9: B

1. C
2. C
3. B
4. A
5. D
6. C
7. B
8. D
9. A
10. 163.28 yd
11. 530.66 ft^2
12. 42 in^2
13. 18 g
14. 1,583 in^2
15. 450 cm^3
16. 470 m^2
17. 494 m^3
18. $7x \geq 370 - 20$

Module Quiz 9: D

1. B
2. C
3. B
4. A
5. A
6. B
7. B
8. C
9. A
10. 50.24 ft
11. 314 ft^2
12. 42 in^2
13. 20 g
14. 264 in^2

15. 438 cm^3
16. 272 m^2
17. 260 m^3
18. $5x \geq 200 - 50$

MODULE 10 Random Samples and Populations

Module Quiz 10: B

1. D
2. A
3. B
4. D
5. B
6. D
7. A
8. C
9. B
10. B
11. Sample answer: Students who ride bikes to school are not represented in the sample. Select 30 students at random in the lunchroom.

Children's Ages

12.
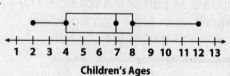
Children's Ages

13.
14. 2-12 years; 7 years
15. 7 years
16. equally likely
17. rectangle, square
18. 500
19. 350
20. 75.36 ft

Module Quiz 10: D

1. B
2. C

3. B

4. C

5. B

6. B

7. A

8. B

9. B

10. B

11. Sample answer: Students who don't ride their bikes are not represented in the survey.

12.

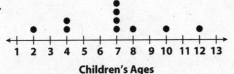

Children's Ages

13. 7 years

14. 2-12 years

15. 7 years

16. more likely to be younger than 8

17. Sample answer: circle

18. 5

19. 25%

20. 75.36 ft

MODULE 11 Analyzing and Comparing Data

Module Quiz 11: B

1. A

2. B

3. B

4. B

5. C

6. B

7. C

8. C

9. science: 78.9%; math: 26.3%

10. science: 3h; math: 4.5 h

11. Math has a higher median (center) and a wider spread.

12. 77.5 for Chapter 9; 65 for Chapter 10

13. ranges: 35 for Chapter 9; 30 for Chapter 10; interquartile ranges: 20 for Chapter 9; 15 for Chapter 10

14. Sample answer: Chapter 10 was considerably more difficult for everyone.

15. 21.7 gal

16. City 1: 68; City 2: 64

17. The difference in the means is 4. The difference of the ranges is 3.

18. 5.25

Module Quiz 11: D

1. A

2. A

3. B

4. A

5. C

6. B

7. C

8. C

9. 1 hour

10. science: 3 hours; math: 4.5 hours

11. science: 5 hours; math: 4 hours

12. 7

13. 95, 80

14. Chapter 10; The median is much lower.

15. 11.5 gal

16. 3

17. The difference in the means is 0.2 times the range.

18. 2.25

MODULE 12 Experimental Probability

Module Quiz 12: B

1. B

2. B

3. D

4. B

5. A

6. C

7. D

8. B

9. D

10. A

11. $\frac{3}{4}$

12. $\frac{146}{158}$ or $\frac{73}{79}$; 0.92

13. $\frac{14}{40}$ or $\frac{7}{20}$; 0.35

14. 9 days

15. 1 h 30 min or 90 min

16. $\frac{28}{55}$ or 0.51

17. 30 more

18. $\frac{4}{9}$

Module Quiz 12: D

1. B
2. B
3. A
4. C
5. A
6. A
7. C
8. A
9. $\frac{5}{7}$
10. 80%
11. $\frac{1}{4}$
12. $\frac{2}{3}$
13. 10
14. $\frac{4}{5}$
15. $\frac{3}{5}$
16. $\frac{1}{3}$
17. $\frac{3}{7}$

MODULE 13 Theoretical Probability and Simulations

Module Quiz 13: B

1. A
2. C
3. A
4. D
5. C
6. A
7. D
8. C
9. C
10. B
11. B
12. D
13. sum of 7; There are more ways for numbers rolled on two number cubes to add up to 7 than to add up to 10.
14. 0.7
15. $40.93
16. 75 min
17. 0.4
18. 5
19. 50

Module Quiz 13: D

1. B
2. A
3. A
4. A
5. B
6. B
7. A
8. A
9. C
10. 10
11. 50
12. 9
13. $\frac{4}{7}$
14. 12
15. $96

16. $\frac{1}{10}$ or 0.1

17. $\frac{4}{7}$

18. 100

Answer Key

Unit Tests and Performance Tasks

UNIT 1 The Number System

Unit 1 Test: A

1. A
2. B
3. D
4. B
5. A
6. C
7. C
8. C
9. C
10. C
11. 31 ft
12. $1\frac{11}{24}$ c
13. −8.5
14. $22.50
15. $140
16. $74
17. 0.9
18. $-1.\overline{3}$
19. $\frac{11}{15}$
20. 130 students
21. Kevin; $5\frac{1}{2} > 5\frac{3}{8}$
22. $\frac{19}{21}$
23. $0.\overline{6}$

Unit 1 Test: B

1. C
2. C
3. D
4. A
5. A
6. A

7. C
8. C
9. C
10. D
11. D
12. C
13. 8.15 fl oz
14. $\frac{5}{8}$
15. 2,625
16. $325
17. $280
18. 165
19. $10.05
20. $-1.3\overline{8}$
21. $102
22. 3.6875 lb
23. 28 questions
24. $\frac{13}{15}$

Unit 1 Test: C

1. D
2. B
3. B
4. D
5. A
6. B
7. A
8. B
9. $3\frac{2}{3}$ mi
10. $4\frac{1}{4}$ lb
11. accept 1 or 1.5
12. $5.42
13. Farmer's market; $\frac{4}{7} > \frac{2}{5}$.
14. $11.50

15. $7\frac{3}{5}$

16. Layla; 20 points higher

17. Science test; $\frac{24}{30} = 0.8$, $\frac{21}{25} = 0.84$

18. $0.76

Unit 1 Test: D

1. C
2. C
3. A
4. C
5. B
6. B
7. A
8. B
9. C
10. B
11. 55
12. $241
13. $\frac{22}{3}$
14. $250
15. 6.75
16. $15
17. −3.5
18. $0.58\overline{3}$
19. 16
20. 10 min
21. $400 loss
22. Yes, the sum is $4.90.
23. $80
24. $-2\frac{2}{3}$

Unit 1 Performance Task

1. 21 + 15 = 36; 36 ft
2. −7.1 − 3.25 = −10.35; −10.35 ft
3. $3 \times 28\frac{3}{4} = 86\frac{1}{4}$; $86\frac{1}{4}$ ft
4. 2.5 x −7.1 = −17.75; at −17.75 ft
5. 86.25 − (−17.75) = 104; 104 ft

6. $2\frac{1}{2}$ x $-6\frac{2}{3} = -16\frac{2}{3}$; at $-16\frac{2}{3}$ ft

7. Answers will vary.

UNIT 2 Ratios and Proportional Relationships

Unit 2 Test: A

1. D
2. B
3. A
4. C
5. B
6. B
7. B
8. B
9. C
10. C
11. $1.62/lb
12. 510 m
13. $y = 2x$
14. 75%
15. $71.25
16. $43.20
17. The ratio between every horizontal and vertical change is the same or constant.
18. $25 per shirt
19. 9 in.
20. Sample answer: Label the horizontal axis hours and the vertical axis miles. Points would be at (1, 60), (2,120), (3,180), and so on. The line connecting the points shows rate of change.

Unit 2 Test: B

1. B
2. D
3. C
4. C
5. B
6. B
7. B
8. B
9. B

10. C

11. 1,440 parts per h

12. $k = 8.5$

13. $y = 4x$

14. From 2000 to 2005, there was a 25.6% decrease. From 2005 to 2010, there was a 75% increase.

15. $403.75

16. $47.93

17. a straight line; the ratio between every horizontal and vertical change is the same or constant.

18. $8 per ticket

19. 190 km

20. Sample answer: Label the horizontal axis seconds and the vertical axis feet. Points would be at (1, 15), (2, 30), (3, 45), and so on. The line connecting the points shows rate of change.

Unit 2 Test: C

1. A
2. B
3. C
4. B
5. D
6. A
7. C
8. B
9. C
10. C

11. 193.55 parts per h

12. $k = 8.5$, $k = 12.5$; The second object is moving faster.

13. $y = 2.5x$

14. 62.5%

15. $23

16. $200 • 115% = $230, the retail price; $230 • 85% = $195.5, the sale price

17. Sample answer: She should draw a straight line with points (0, 0), (1, 4) (2, 8).

18. $1.19 per battery

19. Sample answer: Label the horizontal axis minutes and the vertical axis meters. Points would be at (1, 3.5), (2, 7), (3, 10.5), and so on. The line connecting the points shows rate of change.

20. $3\dfrac{23}{40}$ ft or 42.9 in. or 3 ft 6.9 in.

Unit 2 Test: D

1. A
2. C
3. B
4. C
5. A
6. B
7. A
8. C
9. A
10. C

11. 3; $16\dfrac{2}{3}$ cents

12. 12, 18

13. $18

14. 0.75, 75%

15. 90%, $400, $360

16. $2.00

17. a straight line

18. $9 per book

19. 1,200 mi

20. Sample answer: Label the horizontal axis hours and the vertical axis miles. Points would be at (1, 15), (2, 30), (3, 45), and so on. The line connecting the points shows rate of change.

Unit 2 Performance Task

1. 25; 50; 125; 200

2. and 4.

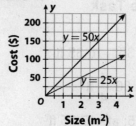

3. $y = 50x$

5.

Size (m²)	0.5	1	2.5	4
Cost ($)	27.50	55.00	137.50	220.00

6. It will get a little steeper.

7. $y = 0.55x$

8.

Size (m²)	0.5	1	2.5	4
Cost ($)	17.50	35.00	87.50	140.00

9. Barkly: $112.53; Woof-Woof: $71.61

UNIT 3 Expressions, Equations, and Inequalities

Unit 3 Test: A

1. D
2. C
3. B
4. B
5. B
6. A
7. A
8. B
9. A
10. A
11. 3 h
12. $x = 4$
13.
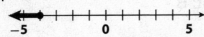
14. −2
15. $75 + 15x$
16. $5
17. $15
18. $y = 5x + 15$
19. $2x + 5 = 25$
20. −17
21. 100 h

Unit 3 Test: B

1. A
2. A
3. D

4. A
5. D
6. A
7. B
8. C
9. D
10. 5 h
11. 12
12.

13. 7
14. $46x - 1000$
15. $102.50
16. $9
17. $3.50
18. $y = 9 + 3.5x$
19. $2
20. 1.5
21. more than $5,000,000

Unit 3 Test: C

1. B
2. A
3. C
4. B
5. B
6. C
7. A
8. A
9. C
10. Mike will earn $5 more.
11. 14
12.

13. −4
14. $w \leq 15$. w must be a positive number
15. $15.75
16. $6.75
17. $y = 15.75 + 6.75x$

18. $0.75

19. $48 + 18 + 8c \le 200$; $c \le 16.75$. He can purchase up to 16 calculators.

Unit 3 Test: D

1. B
2. B
3. A
4. A
5. A
6. B
7. C
8. A
9. A
10. A
11. C
12. 5 h
13. $x > 2$
14.

15. 9
16. $50 + 25x$
17. Sample answer: The values increase by $500 per computer.
18. $2x + 4 = 11$
19. $21.25
20. 32
21. $y > 12x$

Unit 3 Performance Task

1. She pays $35.75 for 75 texts and $35.00 for 50 texts. She pays $35.75 − $35.00 = $0.75 for 25 texts, or $0.75 ÷ 25 = $0.03 per text message.

2. The monthly fee without sending any texts is $35 − 50($0.03) = $33.50.

3. Using the results of Problems 1 and 2, $m = 33.50 + 0.03t$.

4. Set $m = 77$ in the equation above; $77 = 33.5 + 0.03t$, or $0.03t = 43.5$. $t = 1,450$ text messages

5. $33.5 + 0.03t < 80$, or $0.03t < 46.5$; $t < 1,550$.

6. Set $t = 900$ to see how much her current plan costs. $33.5 + 0.03(900) = 60.50. She should keep her plan because it will most likely cost her less.

UNIT 4 Geometry

Unit 4 Test: A

1. C
2. D
3. A
4. B
5. B
6. B
7. C
8. B
9. A
10. 9 in.
11. Students' triangles should have three angles measuring 60° and three side lengths measuring 1 inch.
12. rectangle
13. 110°
14. 282.6 yd
15. 5,024 ft^2
16. 300 in^2
17. 736 ft^2
18. 960 ft^3

Unit 4 Test: B

1. B
2. D
3. C
4. B
5. B
6. C
7. C
8. C
9. A
10. 190 km
11. Students' triangles should have angles measuring 35°, 75° and 70° and side lengths measuring 1 inch, 1 inch and 0.61 inches.

12. pentagon

13. 15°

14. 307.72 yd

15. 6,644.24 ft^2

16. 533 in^2

17. 2,336 ft^2

18. 6,720 ft^3

Unit 4 Test: C

1. A

2. D

3. D

4. B

5. D

6. B

7. C

8. D

9. B

10. Answers will vary. Sample answer: 1 cm : 180 km, then 11 in. will equal 5,029.2 km

11. 94°, 1.1 in. and 1.3 in.

12. Answers will vary. Sample answer:

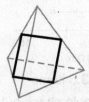

13. No, a tree cannot be planted because the measure of angle A is 180° − (90° −75°), or 15°, which is less than 20°.

14. 22.6 h

15. 8 slices

16. 11 whole pints of paint

17. 24 ft

18. No, the volume of the tent is 6,720 ft^3, so the fan isn't powerful enough to cool the space

Unit 4 Test: D

1. C

2. A

3. C

4. A

5. C

6. A

7. B

8. B

9. C

10. 300 mi

11. no triangle

12. Students' drawings should be in the shape of a rectangle or square.

13. 70°

14. 28.26 yd

15. 50.24 ft^2

16. 75 in^2

17. 992 ft^2

18. 1,920 ft^3

Unit 4 Performance Task

1. circle

2. 153.86 in^2

3. 43.96 in.

4. 120°

5. 487.17 in^2

6. 1,760 in^3

7. 1,216 in^2

8. 30 mi

UNIT 5 Statistics

Unit 5 Test: A

1. C

2. B

3. C

4. B

5. A

6. B

7. C

8. A

9. The mean of the random sample is 5, so the average family size in the neighborhood is estimated to be 5.

10.

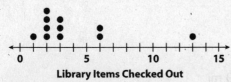

Library Items Checked Out

11. range: 12; median: 3

12. 13 items

13. Yes, the question suggests soccer as a sport.

14.

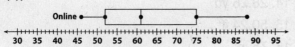

15. In-Store: $52; Online: $61

16. Sample answer: The online buyers tend to spend more.

Unit 5 Test: B

1. B

2. B

3. C

4. D

5. A

6. B

7. C

8. D

9. The mean of the random sample is 5, so the total number of people in the neighborhood is estimated to be 15 × 5, or 75.

10.

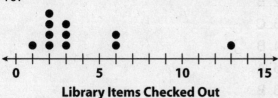

Library Items Checked Out

11. range: 12 items; mode: 2 items; median: 3 items

12. Sample answer: The outlier pulls the mean to the right. It makes the mean higher than is representative of the data.

13. Sample answer: What is your favorite after-school activity?

14.

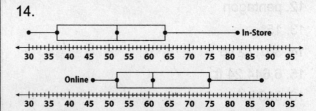

15. In-Store: median $52, range $52; Online: median $61, range $42

16. Sample answers: The online buyers tend to spend more. There is a wider spread for the in-store buyers.

Unit 5 Test: C

1. A

2. A

3. A

4. D

5. D

6. D

7. B

8. C

9. 49,660.8 gal

10.

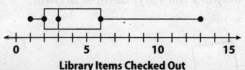

Library Items Checked Out

11. with: 4.23 items; without: 3.5 items

12. Sample answer: Most people check out 2 or 3 items.

13. Sample answer: She should survey random people in her community, not just people walking dogs, since they would likely be in favor of a new dog park.

14.

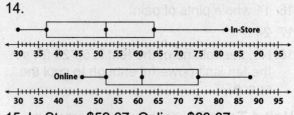

15. In-Store: $52.67, Online: $63.67

16. Sample answers: The online buyers tend to spend more. There is a wider spread for the in-store buyers.

Unit 5 Test: D

1. B
2. B
3. B
4. A
5. C
6. C
7. A
8. C
9. 5
10.

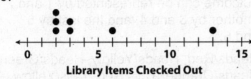

Library Items Checked Out

11. 11 items
12. 3 items
13. yes
14.

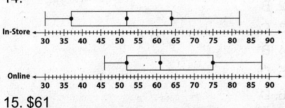

15. $61
16. the online buyers; The median is higher.

Unit 5 Performance Task

1.

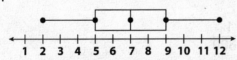

2. Answers will vary depending on student-generated data.

3. Answers will vary depending on student-generated data. It is very unlikely that students will get a symmetrical distribution using such a small number of simulated rolls.

4. Sample answer: We need to simulate a greater number of rolls.

5. range: 9; interquartile range: 5; median: 4.5

6. mean: 4.5

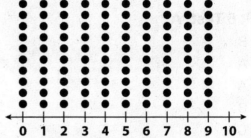

7. Answers will vary depending on student-generated data. Sample answer with an area code of 847

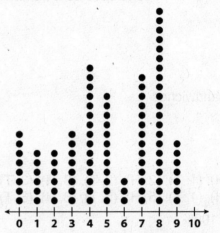

Sample answer: The digits 8, 4, and 7 appear most frequently because all 10 phone numbers have the area code 847

8. Answers will vary depending on student-generated data. Sample answers for dot plot and box plot

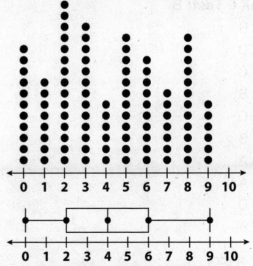

9. Answers will vary depending on student-generated data. Sample answer: The ranges are the same. The median is lower in the cell phone numbers.

UNIT 6 Probability

Unit 6 Test: A

1. B
2. A
3. A
4. B
5. C
6. B
7. C
8. A
9. C
10. B
11. D
12. 12 sandwiches
13. 100
14. $\frac{19}{40}$
15. (1, H), (1, T), (2, H), (2, T), (3, H), (3, T), (4, H), (4, T), (5, H), (5, T), (6, H), (6, T)
16. 1 or 100%
17. $\frac{3}{5}$
18. $\frac{5}{26}$
19. 0

Unit 6 Test: B

1. B
2. D
3. C
4. B
5. C
6. B
7. A
8. A
9. D
10. B
11. $\frac{1}{2,600}$
12. $\frac{55}{96}$
13. $\frac{61}{157}$

14. Answers will vary. Sample answer: Experimental probabilities are based on observations/data. Theoretical probabilities are calculated by finding the total number of desired outcomes and dividing by the total possible outcomes.
15. $\frac{1}{6}$
16. $1 - p$
17. $\frac{7}{30}$
18. Answers will vary. Sample answer: One outcome can be represented by 1 and 2, another by 3 and 4, and the last by 5 and 6.
19. Heads/Red, Heads/Yellow, Heads/Green, Heads/Orange, Tails/Red, Tails/Yellow, Tails/Green, Tails/Orange

Unit 6 Test: C

1. B
2. B
3. C
4. B
5. D
6. D
7. A
8. D
9. C
10. B
11. $\frac{1}{2,600}$
12. 63
13. $\frac{56}{122}$ or $\frac{28}{61}$
14. $\frac{1}{6}$
15. $\frac{1}{9}$
16. $\frac{1}{5}$
17. 32
18. $\frac{1}{5}$ or 20%

Unit 6 Test: D

1. B
2. B
3. B
4. C
5. A
6. B
7. B
8. A
9. 10
10. 30
11. $\frac{1}{6}$
12. $\frac{1}{2}$
13. 6
14. 0
15. $\frac{3}{5}$
16. $\frac{1}{4}$
17. $\frac{1}{3}$

Unit 6 Performance Task

1. The possible outcomes are: red-red, red-green, red-orange, red-blue green-red, green-green, green-orange, green-blue, orange-red, orange-green, orange-orange, orange-blue, blue-red, blue-green, blue-orange, blue-blue

2. 0.25

3. 0.4

4. Answers will vary. Sample answer: Experimental probability is based on previous trials. Theoretical probability is the total number of desired outcomes divided by total possible outcomes.

5. $400 \times 0.25 = 100$ times

6. Answers will vary. Sample answer: 1 and 2 can represent red; 3 and 4 can represent green; 5 and 6 can represent orange; and 7 and 8 can represent blue.

Answer Key
Benchmark Test Modules 1–3

1. A
2. A
3. C
4. C
5. A
6. C
7. B
8. C
9. B
10. A
11. D
12. C
13. D
14. C
15. A
16. B
17. D
18. B
19. C
20. B
21. B
22. D
23. B
24. B
25. A

26. C
27. *A* and *D*
28. $5.84
29. −282 ft
30. $12 per h
31. 130 seashells
32. −$1,280
33. −20 ft/min
34. 9
35. 20
36. 105 meters
37. $3\dfrac{3}{8}$
38. 5.6
39. 4.3 km
40. −16°F

Answer Key

Mid-Year Test Modules 4–7

1. C
2. A
3. C
4. B
5. A
6. B
7. B
8. B
9. C
10. B
11. C
12. C
13. C
14. A
15. B
16. D
17. B
18. A
19. D
20. B
21. D
22. C
23. A
24. C
25. C
26. D
27. B
28. C

29. C
30. $133.90
31. 17 kittens
32. Sample answer: Josh subtracted first when he should have divided first. The answer is 0.
33. $53.65
34. 18 pages
35. Add 16 to each side of the equation.
36. 25%
37. 7 cups
38. $-2x \le -50; x \ge 25$
39. $15.23/day
40. $2x + 8 = 20; x = 6$
41. Sample answer: The graph is a straight line that crosses both axes at the origin.

Answer Key

Benchmark Test Modules 8–11

1. A
2. B
3. B
4. B
5. D
6. A
7. C
8. A
9. B
10. B
11. C
12. B
13. A
14. C
15. B
16. B
17. C
18. D
19. C
20. C
21. D
22. D
23. C
24. B
25. A
26. C
27. D
28. B
29. A
30. D

31. B
32. 47 in.
33. October
34. October
35. Sample answer: He could flip a dime and a penny. If both land the same, you win a pencil. If dime lands heads and penny lands tails, you win a CD. If dime lands tails and penny lands heads, you win a book.
36. 79.3 in^2
37. rectangle
38. The rectangles are congruent.
39. $\frac{3}{4}$ in.:1 ft
40. Check student's sketch; isosceles triangle

Answer Key

End-of-Year Test

1. D
2. D
3. B
4. A
5. A
6. A
7. B
8. B
9. B
10. A
11. C
12. D
13. B
14. B
15. C
16. D
17. B
18. B
19. B
20. D
21. A
22. C
23. B
24. B
25. A
26. C
27. B
28. C
29. D
30. C
31. D
32. C
33. B
34. D
35. D
36. B
37. D
38. C

39. D
40. D
41. A
42. B
43. C
44. A
45. C
46. C
47. D
48. C
49. A
50. B
51. B
52. D
53. C
54. B
55. $81.51
56. 0.6 or 0.60
57. 1.7 h
58. 7 times
59. 13.5 in^3
60. 25 years old
61. 193.79 in^2
62. 8 cups
63. 0.27
64. 150 mi
65. −7
66. 9 cm
67. 85.19 mm
68. $2,581
69. 5
70. 378 m^2
71. 3.93 km
72. 175 in.
73. 8.2 mi^2
74. 1.61 km
75. 0.15

76. $-8\frac{3}{4}$ degrees

77. 3

78. $0.89

79. 10°

80. $\frac{2}{9} = \frac{x}{126}$; $x = 28$

81. 248 in²

82. 8

83. B and D

84. $t \div 0.15$

85. They are congruent rectangles.

86. 0.25

87. Check student's drawing; equilateral triangle

88. Check student's sample space; 6 possible outcomes

89. Use a simulation to generate frequencies of a compound event.

90. Carl is correct; Amber evaluated $(-3)(-2x)$ as $-6x$ instead of $6x$; Butch multiplied $-2x$ by -1 instead of by -3.